Oster

Creative
Countertop Oven
Cooking

Louis Weber, CEO
Publications International, Ltd.
7373 North Cicero Avenue
Lincolnwood, IL 60712

Permission is never granted for commercial purposes.

Distributed by Sunbeam Products, Inc. d/b/a Jarden Consumer Solutions.

Pictured on the front cover: Aztec Brownies (page 122).
Pictured on the back cover: No-Chop Pastitsio (page 26), Sesame-Honey Vegetable Casserole (page 24) and Quick Chocolate Chip Sticky Buns (page 102).

ISBN-13: 978-1-4127-9937-9
ISBN-10: 1-4127-9937-6

Library of Congress Control Number: 2008922220

Manufactured in U.S.A.

8 7 6 5 4 3 2 1

Microwave Cooking: Microwave ovens vary in wattage. Use the cooking times as guidelines and check for doneness before adding more time.

table of contents

Introduction 4

Appetizers 6

Oster® countertop ovens are perfect for cooking up little bites of this or that such as satisfying snacks, creative appetizers, or even light meals.

Casseroles 24

Your **Oster**® countertop oven holds the key to convenient meals; these casseroles are quick, easy, and delicious ways to feed your family.

Vegetable Sides 44

Try whipping up a little something extra with the convenience and flexibility of your **Oster**® countertop oven.

Main Dishes 62

Why waste time and fuel preheating a full-size oven when your food can be cooked perfectly, and maybe even more quickly, by your **Oster**® countertop oven?

Breakfast 82

There's no better way to start your day than with these fresh-baked breakfast treats straight from your **Oster**® countertop oven.

Muffins & Quick Breads 102

The **Oster**® countertop oven easily turns out 6 muffins at a time or a standard loaf of your favorite quick bread.

Cookies, Brownies & Bars 120

Bake up a batch of brownies, or enjoy cookies fresh from the **Oster**® countertop oven.

Cakes, Pies & Tarts 138

The **Oster**® countertop oven can produce delicious, full-size desserts just right to cap off any meal.

Index 156

Metric Conversion Chart 160

Creative Cooking With the Oster® Countertop Oven

Your Countertop Oven Is an "Oven" After All

Sure, it can toast a bagel or reheat a slice of leftover pizza, but have you ever wondered what your countertop oven can *really* do? This cookbook includes many of the exciting possibilities!

Why Use a Countertop Oven?

- **Convenience**: It sits on the counter, offering easier access. There's no need to bend over to slide dishes in or out of the oven.
- **Size**: If you only need to heat up two chicken breasts, six chicken nuggets, or other small meals, now you can avoid heating up the whole kitchen!
- **Speed**: Often there is no preheating required, and typically, food is done in less time than in a conventional oven.
- **Ease**: Because of its size and placement on the counter, it is easier to monitor your food and easier to clean—in most cases, you just pull out the crumb tray and toss the crumbs!

Oster® Countertop Oven Features, A Buyer's Guide

- **Size: Oster® Countertop Ovens** come in many sizes. Pick the one that is right for your counter space. (Please keep in mind that it is recommended that you move the countertop oven out at least 6 inches from the wall while heating.)

- **Capacity**: Are you cooking for two? Or are you cooking for six? Most **Oster® Countertop Ovens** will hold a 9×9-inch casserole dish. Plus, if you see an **Oster® Countertop Oven** with the indication "PIZZA FIT," it can fit a whole large frozen pizza—great for those nights when the kids bring over friends.

- **Functions**: All **Oster® Countertop Ovens** have three basic functions: toast, bake, and broil. Using these, you can cook almost anything. This recipe book contains many creative ideas to get you started!
- **Timer with Automatic Shut-off**: Once the timer bell rings the heating stops—a great safety tool in case you walk away from the kitchen for a moment.
- **Removable Crumb Tray**: When the oven is cool, pull out the crumb tray and easily toss the crumbs away, or wipe off any mess.

Oster® Performance Features*

- **Convection Technology**: When an **Oster® Countertop Oven** is turned to the Convection Bake feature, the oven turns on a fan that circulates the heated air around the food, cooking items evenly and faster.
- **Adjustable Broil**: When an **Oster® Countertop Oven** is turned to Broil, the temperature can be adjusted to between 150°F and 450°F. This allows for great control: Broil at 150°F to melt cheese, broil at 300°F to brown garlic bread, or broil a piece of meat at 450°F.

What's Inside?

This cookbook contains many creative recipes for using your **Oster® Countertop Oven**, from appetizers and snacks to main courses and desserts. You'll find recipes that are sure to impress your friends and family whatever the occasion.

We have included classic recipes as well as some recipes with a few new twists, all of which can be prepared in your **Oster® Countertop Oven**. There are a variety of excellent seasonal ideas and exciting ethnic dishes, too!

Whether you're warming up a savory snack or baking a delicious peach cobbler, your **Oster® Countertop Oven** can do more than you ever imagined. Once you see all that your **Oster® Countertop Oven** can do, you'll want to create your own signature dishes to add to your repertoire!

*Performance features not available on all models; check instruction manual to verify availability.

appetizers

Spicy Glazed Pecans

1 cup pecan halves	¼ teaspoon ground cumin
1 teaspoon salt	⅛ teaspoon ground red pepper
1 teaspoon chili powder	¼ cup sugar
1 teaspoon olive oil	¼ cup beer

1. Preheat **Oster® Countertop Oven** to 350°F. Line oven tray with foil.

2. Mix pecans, salt, chili powder, olive oil, cumin and red pepper in small bowl. Spread onto prepared tray. Toast 10 minutes or until nuts are fragrant. Cool in pan on wire rack.

3. Combine sugar and beer in small saucepan. Heat over medium-high heat until mixture registers 250°F on candy thermometer. Remove from heat; carefully stir in nuts and any loose spices. Spread sugared nuts on foil-lined oven tray, separating clusters.

4. Let cool. Break up any large pieces before serving.

Makes 1½ cups

Zucchini Pizza Bites

⅓ **cup salsa**

2 **small zucchini, trimmed and cut diagonally into ¼-inch-thick slices**

¼ **pound fresh chorizo sausage***

6 **tablespoons shredded reduced-fat mozzarella cheese**

*Chorizo is a spicy pork sausage used in both Mexican and Spanish cooking. The Mexican variety (which is more widely available in the U.S.) is a fresh sausage that must be cooked before it is eaten while the Spanish variety is smoked and dried and may be eaten as sold.

1. Preheat **Oster® Countertop Oven** to 400°F. Place salsa in fine sieve and press out excess moisture; set aside to drain. Remove sausage from casing; crumble into small skillet. Cook and stir 5 minutes or until cooked through; drain fat.

2. Place zucchini on oven tray. Spoon 1 teaspoon drained salsa on each zucchini slice. Top with chorizo, dividing evenly among zucchini slices. Sprinkle 1½ teaspoons cheese over each slice.

3. Bake 10 minutes or until cheese is lightly browned. Serve immediately.

Makes 6 servings

Bacon-Wrapped Glazed Chicken

**4 chicken tender strips, patted dry
(about ½ pound)**

**¼ teaspoon paprika or ground
cumin (optional)**

4 slices bacon

¼ cup barbecue sauce, divided

1. Preheat broiler in **Oster® Countertop Oven.** Line oven tray with foil; set aside.

2. Sprinkle chicken strips with paprika. Wrap each chicken strip with 1 slice of bacon in spiral pattern; place on baking tray.

3. Broil chicken 4 minutes. Turn chicken over; broil 2 minutes more. Remove from countertop oven; brush with ¼ cup barbecue sauce. Broil 2 minutes. Remove from oven.

Makes 2 servings

Aegean Feta Bruchetta

**6 slices feta cheese
(about 2 ounces total)**

1 onion, cut into ¼-inch-thick slices

**¼ green bell pepper, seeded and
cut into strips**

**¼ red bell pepper, seeded and cut
into strips**

Pinch dried oregano

**Garlic pepper or black pepper
(optional)**

**6 (½-inch-thick) slices French
bread**

1. Preheat **Oster® Countertop Oven** to 400°F. Spray 14-inch-long sheet of foil with nonstick cooking spray.

2. Place 6 onion slices in center of foil and top with feta slices (reserve remaining onion for another use). Sprinkle with bell pepper strips and oregano. Add garlic pepper, if desired. Bring two long sides of foil together above food; fold down in a series of locked folds, allowing for heat circulation and expansion. Fold short ends up and over again. Press folds firmly to seal foil packet.

3. Place foil packet in countertop oven; cook 20 minutes. Open packet carefully. Serve immediately with French bread slices.

Makes 2 servings

Sausage-Stuffed Mushrooms

4 ounces uncooked turkey Italian sausage, casings removed

2 tablespoons plain dry bread crumbs

4 medium portobello mushroom caps

1 tablespoon olive oil

¼ cup grated Asiago cheese

1. Preheat **Oster® Countertop Oven** to 325°F. Crumble sausage into small skillet. Cook over medium-high heat until no longer pink; drain fat. Remove from heat; stir in bread crumbs.

2. Brush both sides of mushroom caps lightly with oil. Spoon sausage mixture evenly into mushroom caps.

3. Place mushrooms, stuffing side up, on oven tray. Sprinkle with cheese. Bake 15 minutes or until cheese melts and mushrooms are tender.

Makes 4 servings

Apple and Cheese Pockets

1 medium to large Golden Delicious apple, peeled, cored and finely chopped (1 cup)

1 cup shredded sharp Cheddar cheese

1 tablespoon apple jelly

Pinch curry powder

4 large reduced-fat refrigerated biscuits (2 ounces each)

1. Preheat **Oster® Countertop Oven** to 350°F. Line oven tray with parchment paper; set aside.

2. Combine apples, cheese, apple jelly and curry powder in large bowl and stir well.

3. Roll out one biscuit on lightly floured surface to 6½-inch circle. Place ½ cup apple mixture in center. Fold biscuit over filling to form a semicircle; press to seal tightly. Place on oven tray. Repeat with remaining biscuits and filling. Bake 15 to 18 minutes or until biscuits are golden and filling is hot. Cool slightly then serve. Or cool completely and refrigerate in airtight container until serving. Reheat in microwave about 30 seconds on HIGH until hot.

Makes 4 servings

Note: Refrigerate up to two days or freeze up to one month after baking.

Coconut Chicken Tenders with Spicy Mango Salsa

½ firm ripe mango, peeled, seeded and chopped

¼ cup chopped red bell pepper

1½ tablespoons chopped green onion

1 tablespoon chopped fresh cilantro

Salt and ground red pepper

¾ cup flaked coconut

1 egg

1 tablespoon vegetable oil

½ pound chicken tenders

1. Combine mango, bell pepper, onion and cilantro in small bowl. Season to taste with salt and ground red pepper. Transfer half of salsa to food processor; process until finely chopped (almost puréed). Combine with remaining salsa.

2. Preheat **Oster® Countertop Oven** to 400°F. Spread coconut on oven tray. Bake 3 to 4 minutes or until lightly browned, stirring every minute. Transfer coconut to food processor; process until finely chopped but not pasty.

3. Beat egg with oil and pinch of ground red pepper in small bowl. Add chicken tenders; toss to coat. Roll tenders in coconut; arrange on foil-lined oven tray. Bake 18 to 20 minutes or until no longer pink in center. Serve with mango salsa.

Makes 5 to 6 servings

Spiced Halibut, Pineapple and Pepper Skewers

1 tablespoon lemon juice or lime juice

½ teaspoon minced garlic

½ teaspoon chili powder

¼ teaspoon ground cumin

Pinch of ground cinnamon

Pinch of ground cloves

¼ pound boneless, skinless halibut steak, about 1 inch thick

¼ small pineapple, peeled, halved lengthwise and cut into 12 pieces

½ large green or red bell pepper, cut into 12 pieces

1. Combine lemon juice, garlic, chili powder, cumin, cinnamon and cloves in large resealable food storage bag; knead until blended.

2. Rinse fish; pat dry. Cut into 6 (1- to 1¼-inch) cubes. Add fish to bag. Press out air; seal. Turn gently to coat fish with marinade. Refrigerate 30 minutes to 1 hour. Soak 6 (6- to 8-inch) wooden skewers in water while fish marinates.

3. Alternately thread 2 pieces pepper, 2 pieces pineapple and 1 piece fish onto each skewer.

4. Preheat broiler in **Oster® Countertop Oven.** Line oven tray with foil; insert broiler rack. Spray broiler rack with nonstick cooking spray. Place skewers on rack. Broil 3 to 4 minutes. Turn skewers over; broil 3 to 4 minutes more or until fish begins to flake when tested with fork.

Makes 3 servings

Apricot BBQ Glazed Shrimp and Bacon

12 water chestnut slices

12 medium raw shrimp, peeled and deveined

3 slices bacon, each cut into 4 pieces

2 scant tablespoons barbecue sauce

2 scant tablespoons apricot fruit spread

1 teaspoon grated fresh ginger

1 teaspoon cider vinegar

Pinch of red pepper flakes

1. Preheat broiler in **Oster® Countertop Oven.** Place 1 water chestnut slice on top of each shrimp. Wrap 1 piece of bacon around shrimp and water chestnut; secure with toothpick. Repeat with remaining water chestnuts, shrimp and bacon.

2. Line oven tray with foil; insert broiler rack. Coat broiler rack with nonstick cooking spray. Place shrimp on rack.

3. Combine barbecue sauce, fruit spread, ginger, vinegar and pepper flakes in small bowl. Brush sauce evenly over appetizers. Broil 2 minutes; turn. Baste and broil 2 minutes more; turn again. Baste and broil 1 minute or until bacon begins to brown.

Makes 12 appetizers

Salmon Wontons with Ginger Soy Sauce

6 tablespoons soy sauce, divided

¼ cup minced peeled fresh ginger (reserve 2 teaspoons ginger)

¼ cup rice vinegar

3 tablespoons honey

½ pound salmon, cut into ½-inch dice

¾ cup finely chopped onion

1 large egg

1 teaspoon minced garlic

¼ teaspoon red pepper flakes chilies

¼ cup sliced green onions

Salt

1 package (12 ounces) wonton wrappers

Blended oil (canola and vegetable) for frying

1. Blend 4 tablespoons soy sauce, ¼ cup (less 2 teaspoons) ginger, rice vinegar and honey in small bowl. Set Ginger Soy Sauce aside.

2. Combine salmon, onion, egg, garlic, red pepper flakes, scallions and salt in medium bowl. Mix in remaining 2 tablespoons soy sauce and remaining 2 teaspoons ginger.

3. Place several wrappers on work surface; brush edges lightly with water. Place heaping 1 teaspoon salmon filling in center of each. Fold wrappers diagonally in half, pressing edges to seal. Place wontons on waxed paper. Repeat with remaining wrappers and filling.

4. Preheat **Oster® Countertop Oven** to 250°F.

5. Heat 1 teaspoon oil in heavy large skillet over medium heat; add one-fourth of wontons. Fry until wontons are golden on bottom, about 3 minutes. Turn over and cook until other side is golden on bottom. Transfer to baking tray; bake in prepared oven until cooked through. Keep warm in oven until serving.

6. Meanwhile, fry remaining wontons, using 1 teaspoon oil per batch. Serve wontons with Ginger Soy Sauce.

Makes 8 servings

Sweet & Savory Brie in Puff Pastry

2 sheets frozen puff pastry

2 (6-inch) Brie rounds

Savory Filling

½ cup green olives

½ cup parsley leaves

1 clove garlic

1 tablespoon olive oil

½ cup packed spinach leaves

Sweet Filling

1 cup whole fresh cranberries

¾ cup dark brown sugar

½ cup pecans

1 teaspoon butter

1. Defrost puff pastry sheets; unfold and place each sheet in a round baking dish that will hold Brie rounds snugly.

2. Remove white skin from tops of Brie rounds. Place each Brie in center of 1 sheet pastry. Fold edges of each pastry over and crimp together to form edge around side of Brie.

3. Combine all ingredients for Savory Filling in food processor; pulse until finely chopped. (Do not overprocess; filling should not form paste.) Spread on top of one Brie round. Combine all ingredients for Sweet Filling in food processor; pulse until finely chopped. (Do not overprocess; should not form a paste.) Spread on top of other Brie round.

4. Preheat **Oster® Countertop Oven** to 400°F. Bake Bries 1 at a time 15 minutes or until pastry is golden. Serve immediately. Accompany with crackers, bread and fruit.

Makes 12 to 14 servings

Sesame-Honey Vegetable Casserole

1 package (16 ounces) frozen mixed vegetable medley, such as baby carrots, broccoli, onions and red bell peppers, thawed and drained

3 tablespoons honey

1 tablespoon dark sesame oil

1 tablespoon soy sauce

2 teaspoons sesame seeds

1. Preheat **Oster® Countertop Oven** to 350°F.

2. Place vegetables in shallow 1½-quart casserole dish. Combine honey, sesame oil, soy sauce and sesame seeds in small bowl; stir until well blended. Drizzle evenly over vegetables. Bake 20 to 25 minutes or until vegetables are tender and hot, stirring after 15 minutes.

Makes 4 servings

No-Chop Pastitsio

1 pound 90% lean ground beef or ground lamb	8 ounces uncooked elbow macaroni
1½ cups mild picante sauce	3 tablespoons butter
1 can (8 ounces) tomato sauce	3 tablespoons all-purpose flour
1 tablespoon sugar	1½ cups milk
½ teaspoon ground allspice	½ teaspoon salt
½ teaspoon ground cinnamon	¼ teaspoon black pepper
¼ teaspoon ground nutmeg, divided	2 eggs, beaten
	½ cup grated Parmesan cheese

1. Preheat **Oster® Countertop Oven** to 350°F. Lightly coat 9-inch square baking dish with nonstick cooking spray; set aside.

2. Brown beef in large skillet over medium-high heat, stirring to break up meat. Drain fat. Add picante sauce, tomato sauce, sugar, allspice, cinnamon and ⅛ teaspoon nutmeg. Bring to a boil; reduce heat and simmer, uncovered, 10 minutes, stirring frequently.

3. Meanwhile, cook macaroni according to package directions; drain. Place in prepared baking dish.

4. Melt butter in medium saucepan over medium heat. Add flour; mix until smooth. Add milk; cook and stir until thickened. Remove from heat. Add about ½ cup white sauce mixture to eggs; stir to blend thoroughly. Add egg mixture to remaining white sauce in saucepan. Stir in Parmesan cheese.

5. Mix about ½ cup white sauce into macaroni; toss to coat completely. Spread meat sauce over macaroni. Top with remaining white sauce. Sprinkle evenly with remaining ⅛ teaspoon nutmeg. Bake, uncovered, 30 to 40 minutes or until knife inserted into center comes out clean. Let stand 15 to 20 minutes before serving.

Makes 6 servings

Midweek Moussaka

1 eggplant (about 1 pound), cut into ¼-inch slices

2 tablespoons olive oil

1 pound 90% lean ground beef

1 can (about 14 ounces) stewed tomatoes, drained

¼ cup red wine

2 tablespoons tomato paste

2 teaspoons sugar

¾ teaspoon salt

½ teaspoon dried oregano

¼ teaspoon ground cinnamon

¼ teaspoon black pepper

⅛ teaspoon ground allspice

4 ounces cream cheese

¼ cup milk

¼ cup grated Parmesan cheese

Ground cinnamon (optional)

1. Preheat broiler in **Oster® Countertop Oven.** Spray 8-inch square baking dish with nonstick cooking spray; set aside.

2. Line oven tray with foil. Arrange eggplant slices on foil; overlap slices slightly if necessary. Brush with olive oil; broil 5 to 6 inches from heat source 4 minutes on each side. Reduce temperature to 350°F.

3. Meanwhile, brown beef in large skillet over medium-high heat, stirring to break up meat. Drain and discard drippings. Add tomatoes, wine, tomato paste, sugar, salt, oregano, cinnamon, pepper and allspice. Bring to a boil, breaking up large pieces of tomato with a spoon. Reduce heat and cover; simmer 10 minutes.

4. Place cream cheese and milk in small microwavable bowl. Cover with plastic wrap; microwave on HIGH 1 minute.* Stir with fork until smooth.

5. Arrange half of eggplant slices in prepared baking dish. Spoon half of meat sauce over eggplant. Sprinkle with half of Parmesan cheese. Repeat layers. Spoon cream cheese mixture evenly on top. Bake 20 minutes or until top begins to crack slightly. Sprinkle lightly with cinnamon, if desired. Let stand 10 minutes before serving.

Makes 4 servings

*Or place in small saucepan over medium heat and stir until cheese has melted.

Home-Style Shepherd's Pie

½ pound 90% lean ground beef

½ pound mild Italian sausage, casings removed

1 cup chopped onion

2 cups frozen mixed vegetables, thawed

1 can (6 ounces) tomato paste

1 tablespoon beef bouillon granules

1 cup water

2 teaspoons sugar

⅛ teaspoon ground red pepper

¼ teaspoon salt

¼ teaspoon black pepper

¼ cup chopped fresh parsley

1 package (2 pounds) refrigerated prepared mashed potatoes

½ cup chopped green onions

¾ cup (about 3 ounces) grated sharp Cheddar cheese

1. Preheat **Oster® Countertop Oven** to 350°F. Lightly coat 2-quart casserole with nonstick cooking spray; set aside.

2. Coat large skillet with cooking spray and heat over medium-high heat until hot. Add beef, sausage and onion; cook until browned, stirring frequently to break up meat. Drain and discard drippings. Add vegetables, tomato paste, bouillon, water, sugar, red pepper, salt, black pepper and parsley; stir until well blended.

3. Transfer mixture to prepared baking dish. Spoon potatoes evenly over all. Sprinkle with green onions. Top with cheese. Coat sheet of foil with cooking spray. Cover dish, sprayed side down, to prevent cheese from sticking. Bake 22 to 25 minutes or until bubbly.

Makes 6 to 8 servings

Shrimp and Chicken Paella

¾ **cup cooked rice**

2 **cans (about 14 ounces each) low-sodium diced tomatoes, undrained**

½ **teaspoon ground turmeric or 1 pinch saffron threads**

1 **package (12 ounces) frozen peeled, deveined shrimp, thawed (about 3 cups)**

2 **chicken tenders (about 4 ounces), cut into bite-size chunks**

1 **cup frozen peas, thawed**

1. Preheat **Oster® Countertop Oven** to 400°F. Lightly coat 8-inch square glass baking dish with nonstick cooking spray.

2. Place rice into baking dish in even layer. Empty 1 can of tomatoes with juice over rice; sprinkle turmeric over tomatoes. Arrange shrimp and chicken over tomatoes. Top with peas.

3. Drain second can of tomatoes; discard juice. Arrange tomatoes evenly over shrimp and chicken. Cover casserole with foil. Bake 30 minutes. Remove from oven and let stand, covered, 5 minutes.

4. To serve, spoon into shallow, rimmed bowls.

Makes 6 servings

Tip: Serve with a green salad tossed with mustard vinaigrette and garnished with ½ cup drained, no-salt-added canned corn.

Festive Corn Casserole

2 cups grated zucchini

1 cup frozen corn

1 cup diced red bell pepper

2 cups cholesterol-free egg substitute

½ cup fat-free evaporated milk

2 teaspoons sugar

¼ teaspoon celery seed

⅛ teaspoon salt

⅛ teaspoon red pepper flakes (optional)

1. Preheat **Oster® Countertop Oven** to 350°F. Coat 2-quart baking dish with nonstick cooking spray.

2. Mix zucchini, corn and bell pepper in baking dish. Whisk egg substitute, evaporated milk, sugar, celery seed, salt and red pepper flakes, if desired, in large bowl; pour over vegetables in baking dish. Bake 45 to 55 minutes or until golden.

Makes 10 servings

Zucchini Tomato Bake

1 pound eggplant, coarsely chopped (4 cups total)

2 cups sliced zucchini

2 cups sliced fresh mushrooms

2 teaspoons olive oil

½ cup chopped onion

½ cup chopped fennel bulb (optional)

2 cloves garlic, minced

1 can (about 14 ounces) whole tomatoes, undrained

1 tablespoon tomato paste

2 teaspoons dried basil

1 teaspoon sugar

1. Preheat **Oster® Countertop Oven** to 400°F.

2. Arrange eggplant, zucchini and mushrooms in 9-inch square baking dish. Heat oil in small skillet over medium heat. Add onion, fennel, if desired, and garlic; cook and stir 3 to 4 minutes or until onion is tender. Add tomatoes with liquid, tomato paste, basil and sugar. Cook and stir about 4 minutes or until sauce thickens.

3. Pour sauce over vegetables. Cover; bake 30 minutes or until vegetables are tender.

Makes 6 servings

Baked Risotto with Asparagus, Spinach & Parmesan

1½ teaspoons olive oil

½ cup finely chopped onion

½ cup arborio rice

4 cups (4 to 5 ounces) packed torn stemmed spinach

1 cup chicken broth

⅛ teaspoon salt

⅛ teaspoon ground nutmeg

½ cup grated Parmesan cheese, divided

¾ cups diagonally sliced asparagus

1. Preheat **Oster® Countertop Oven** to 400°F. Spray 2-quart baking dish with nonstick cooking spray.

2. Heat olive oil in large skillet over medium-high heat. Add onion; cook and stir 4 minutes or until tender. Add rice; stir to coat with oil.

3. Stir in spinach, a handful at a time, adding more as it wilts. Add broth, salt and nutmeg. Reduce heat and simmer 7 minutes. Stir in ¼ cup cheese.

4. Transfer to prepared baking dish. Cover tightly; bake 15 minutes.

5. Remove from oven; stir in asparagus. Sprinkle with remaining ¼ cup cheese. Cover; bake 15 minutes or until liquid is absorbed.

Makes 2 to 4 entrée or 5 to 6 side-dish servings

Carrie's Sweet Potato Casserole

Topping (recipe follows)

1½ pounds sweet potatoes, cooked and peeled*

¼ cup (½ stick) butter, softened

¼ cup sugar

¼ cup evaporated milk

1 egg

½ teaspoon vanilla

½ cup chopped pecans

*For faster preparation, substitute canned sweet potatoes.

1. Preheat **Oster® Countertop Oven** to 350°F. Grease 8 (6-ounce) ovenproof ramekins. Prepare Topping; set aside.

2. Mash sweet potatoes and butter in large bowl. Beat with electric mixer at medium speed until light and fluffy. Add sugar, evaporated milk, eggs and vanilla, beating after each addition. Spread evenly in prepared ramekins. Spoon Topping over potatoes; sprinkle with pecans.

3. Bake 20 to 25 minutes or until set.

Makes 4 servings

Topping

Combine ½ cup packed brown sugar, ¼ cup all-purpose flour and 2½ tablespoons melted butter in medium bowl; mix well.

Chile-Corn Quiche

1 (9-inch) pie crust, 1½ inches deep

1 can (8¾ ounces) corn, drained, or 1 cup frozen corn, cooked

1 can (4 ounces) diced mild green chiles, drained

¼ cup thinly sliced green onions

1 cup (4 ounces) shredded Monterey Jack cheese

3 eggs

1½ cups half-and-half

½ teaspoon salt

½ teaspoon ground cumin

1. Preheat **Oster® Countertop Oven** to 450°F. Line pie crust with foil; partially fill with uncooked beans or rice to weight crust. Bake 10 minutes. Remove foil and beans; continue baking crust 5 minutes or until lightly browned. Let cool. Reduce oven temperature to 375°F.

2. Combine corn, green chiles and green onions in small bowl. Spoon into pie crust; top with cheese. Whisk eggs, half-and-half, salt and cumin in medium bowl. Pour over cheese. Bake 35 to 45 minutes or until filling is puffed and knife inserted into center comes out clean. Let stand 10 minutes to set before serving.

Makes 6 servings

Curried Chicken Pot Pies

1 tablespoon canola oil

¾ cup chopped, peeled Granny Smith apple

⅓ cup thinly sliced carrot

¼ cup chopped onion

1 clove garlic, minced

1 tablespoon all-purpose flour

½ teaspoon curry powder

⅛ teaspoon salt

⅛ teaspoon black pepper

Pinch ground cloves

¾ cup water

1 cup chopped cooked chicken breast

½ cup no-salt-added diced tomatoes, undrained

2 tablespoons minced fresh cilantro

4 refrigerated soft breadsticks

Additional minced fresh cilantro (optional)

1. Preheat **Oster® Countertop Oven** to 375°F. Spray 2 (1½-cup) casseroles or ovenproof bowls with nonstick cooking spray.

2. Heat oil in medium skillet over medium heat. Add apple, carrot, onion and garlic. Cook and stir 3 to 4 minutes or until apple and onion are tender. Add flour, curry powder, salt, pepper and cloves. Cook and stir over medium heat 1 minute. Stir in water. Cook, stirring constantly, until liquid boils and thickens. Stir in chicken and tomatoes. Cook 3 to 4 minutes or until heated through. Stir in 2 tablespoons cilantro. Spoon into prepared casseroles.

3. Arrange 2 breadsticks over top of chicken mixture in each casserole. Sprinkle additional cilantro over tops, if desired.

4. Bake 15 to 17 minutes or until breadsticks are browned and filling is bubbly.

Makes 2 servings

Note: Leftover breadstick dough can be refrigerated in an airtight container and reserved for another use.

Green Chile-Chicken Casserole

2 cups shredded cooked chicken

¾ cup green enchilada sauce

½ can (about 5 ounces) condensed cream of chicken soup, undiluted

½ container (4 ounces) sour cream

½ can (about 2 ounces) diced mild green chiles

¼ cup vegetable oil

6 (6-inch) corn tortillas

¾ cup (6 ounces) shredded Colby-Jack cheese, divided

1. Preheat **Oster® Countertop Oven** to 325°F. Spray 2-quart casserole with nonstick cooking spray.

2. Combine chicken, enchilada sauce, soup, sour cream and chiles in large skillet. Cook and stir over medium-high heat until warm.

3. Heat oil in separate deep skillet. Fry tortillas just until soft; drain on paper towels. Place 2 tortillas on bottom of prepared casserole. Layer with one-third of chicken mixture and ¼ cup cheese. Repeat layers twice.

4. Bake 15 to 20 minutes or until cheese is melted and casserole is heated through.

Makes 2 to 4 servings

Tip: Shredded Mexican cheese blend can be substituted for Colby-Jack cheese.

Triple-Pepper Tomato Provolone Lasagna

1 red bell pepper, chopped

1 yellow bell pepper, chopped

1 green bell pepper, chopped

1 package (8 ounces) sliced fresh mushrooms

1 cup thinly sliced zucchini

½ cup chopped onion

4 cloves garlic, minced

1½ cups vegetable juice cocktail

1 can (16 ounces) diced tomatoes, undrained

1½ to 1¾ teaspoons Italian seasoning

1 tablespoon olive oil

9 uncooked lasagna noodles

1 cup fat-free cottage cheese

⅓ cup grated Parmesan cheese

4 ounces sliced reduced-fat provolone cheese

1. Preheat **Oster® Countertop Oven** to 350°F. Combine peppers, mushrooms, zucchini, onion, garlic, vegetable juice cocktail, tomatoes and Italian seasoning in Dutch oven. Bring to a boil over high heat. Reduce heat to low; simmer, uncovered, 15 minutes. Remove from heat; stir in oil.

2. Spray 8-inch square baking dish with nonstick cooking spray. Place 3 lasagna noodles on bottom of pan. Spread one-third sauce over noodles. Spread ½ cup cottage cheese evenly over sauce; sprinkle with 2 tablespoons Parmesan cheese. Repeat layers, ending with sauce.

3. Bake, uncovered, 1 hour or until bubbly. Tear provolone cheese in small pieces; place on top of lasagna. Sprinkle with remaining Parmesan cheese. Bake 5 minutes longer or until cheese is melted. Let stand 15 minutes. Cut into 6 wedges to serve.

Makes 6 servings

Tip: For extra convenience, purchase 3 cups chopped red, green and yellow bell pepper mixture from the grocery store salad bar.

vegetable sides

Oven-Roasted Asparagus

1 bunch (12 to 14 ounces)
  asparagus spears

1 tablespoon olive oil

½ teaspoon salt

¼ teaspoon black pepper

¼ cup shredded Asiago or
  Parmesan cheese (optional)

1. Preheat **Oster® Countertop Oven** to 425°F.

2. Trim off and discard tough ends of asparagus spears. Peel stem ends with vegetable peeler, if desired. Arrange asparagus in oven tray; drizzle with oil, turning spears to coat. Sprinkle with salt and pepper.

3. Roast asparagus until tender, about 12 to 18 minutes depending on thickness of asparagus. Chop or leave spears whole. Sprinkle with cheese, if desired.

Makes 4 servings

Veggies and Couscous

⅓ cup pine nuts

1½ cups chicken broth or water

½ teaspoon salt

1 tablespoon olive oil, plus more for basting vegetables

1 cup couscous

1 medium zucchini, cut lengthwise into ½-inch slices

1 medium red bell pepper, cut in half

½ small red onion, sliced

¼ cup crumbled feta or basil-tomato flavored feta cheese

1 clove garlic, minced

½ teaspoon lemon pepper

Salt and black pepper

1. Toast pine nuts in small nonstick skillet over medium heat 5 minutes or until just brown and fragrant. Cool; set aside.

2. Place broth, ½ teaspoon salt and olive oil in small saucepan; bring to a boil. Stir in couscous. Cover; remove from heat. Set aside.

3. Preheat broiler in **Oster® Countertop Oven.** Brush vegetables with olive oil. Place zucchini and onion on oven tray; roast 3 to 5 minutes or until tender. Roast bell pepper 7 to 10 minutes or until skin is blackened. When bell pepper is blackened, place in small plastic bag; seal and set aside 3 to 5 minutes. Remove from bag; peel off blackened skin. Dice vegetables.

4. Spoon couscous into serving bowl. Fluff with fork. Add diced vegetables, toasted pine nuts, feta cheese, garlic and lemon pepper; mix well. Sprinkle to taste with salt and black pepper.

Makes 6 servings

Corn Pudding

1 tablespoon butter	¾ teaspoon salt
1 small onion, chopped	¼ teaspoon black pepper
1 tablespoon all-purpose flour	¼ teaspoon hot pepper sauce
2 cups half-and-half	2 cups corn
1 cup milk	1 can (4 ounces) diced mild green chiles, drained
¼ cup quick-cooking grits or polenta	4 eggs, lightly beaten

1. Preheat **Oster® Countertop Oven** to 325°F. Grease 11×7-inch baking dish.

2. Melt butter in large saucepan over medium heat. Add onion; cook and stir 5 minutes or until tender and light golden. Stir in flour; cook until golden. Stir in half-and-half and milk. Bring to a boil. Whisk in grits; reduce heat to medium-low. Cook and stir 10 minutes or until mixture is thickened.

3. Remove from heat. Stir in salt, black pepper and hot pepper sauce. Add corn and chiles. Stir in eggs. Pour into prepared dish. Bake 1 hour or until knife inserted into center comes out clean.

Makes 8 servings

Potluck tip: *If prepared in advance, bake pudding in glass baking dish as directed. Cover and refrigerate up to one day. To serve, microwave at your host's home until heated through. Or wrap baked dish in several layers of foil and overwrap with thick towel or newspapers to keep finished dish warm when transporting.*

Tricolored Pepper Salad

1 each large red, yellow and green bell pepper, cut into halves or quarters

⅓ cup extra-virgin olive oil

3 tablespoons balsamic vinegar

2 cloves garlic, minced

¼ teaspoon salt

¼ teaspoon black pepper

⅓ cup crumbled goat cheese (about 1½ ounces)

¼ cup thinly sliced fresh basil leaves

1. Preheat broiler in **Oster® Countertop Oven.**

2. Place bell peppers skin-side down on oven tray. Roast bell peppers, covered, 8 to 10 minutes or until skin is charred. Place charred bell peppers in paper bag. Close bag; set aside to cool 10 to 15 minutes. Remove skin; discard.

3. Place bell peppers in shallow glass serving dish. Combine oil, vinegar, garlic, salt and black pepper in small bowl; whisk until well combined. Pour over bell peppers. Let stand 30 minutes at room temperature. (Or cover and refrigerate up to 24 hours. Bring bell peppers to room temperature before serving.)

4. Sprinkle bell peppers with cheese and basil just before serving.

Makes 4 to 6 servings

Poblano Pepper Kabobs

1 large poblano pepper*

4 ounces smoked turkey breast, cut into 8 cubes

4 ounces pepper-jack cheese, cut into 8 cubes

¼ cup salsa (optional)

Poblano peppers can sting and irritate the skin, so wear rubber gloves when handling peppers and do not touch your eyes.

1. Preheat **Oster® Countertop Oven** to 400°F. Fill medium saucepan half full with water; bring to a boil over medium-high heat. Add pepper; cook 1 minute. Drain. Core, seed and cut pepper into 12 bite-size pieces.

2. Soak 4 wooden skewers in warm water 20 minutes to prevent burning. Thread 1 piece pepper, 1 piece turkey and 1 piece cheese onto each of 4 skewers. Repeat, ending with pepper.

3. Place kabobs on oven tray. Bake 3 minutes or until cheese starts to melt. Serve with salsa, if desired.

Makes 4 servings

Mediterranean Roasted Tomatoes

2 small to medium beefsteak tomatoes, cut in half crosswise

4 fresh basil leaves

2 tablespoons finely chopped pitted kalamata olives

2 tablespoons shredded reduced-fat mozzarella cheese

2 tablespoons grated Parmesan cheese

1. Preheat **Oster® Countertop Oven** to broil. Place tomato halves on oven tray. Top each tomato half with 1 fresh basil leaf, one-fourth of olives, one-fourth of mozzarella and one-fourth of Parmesan.

2. Broil 2 minutes or until cheese melts and begins to brown. Let cool slightly before serving.

Makes 4 servings

Oven "Fries"

2 small baking potatoes

2 teaspoons olive oil

¼ teaspoon salt or onion salt

1. Place potatoes in refrigerator 1 to 2 days.

2. Preheat **Oster® Countertop Oven** to 450°F. Peel potatoes and cut lengthwise into ¼-inch-square strips. Place in colander. Rinse potato strips under cold running water 2 minutes. Drain. Pat dry with paper towels. Place potatoes in small resealable food storage bag. Drizzle with oil. Seal bag; shake to coat potatoes with oil.

3. Arrange potatoes in single layer on oven tray. Bake 20 to 25 minutes or until light brown and crisp. Sprinkle with salt or onion salt.

Makes 2 servings

Note: Refrigerating potatoes—usually not recommended for storage—converts starch in the potatoes to sugar, which enhances the browning when the potatoes are baked. Do not refrigerate the potatoes longer than 2 days or they might begin to taste sweet.

Oven-Roasted Potatoes and Onions with Herbs

3 pounds unpeeled red potatoes, cut into 1½-inch cubes

1 large sweet onion, such as Vidalia or Walla Walla, coarsely chopped

3 tablespoons olive oil

2 tablespoons butter, melted, or bacon drippings

3 cloves garlic, minced

¾ teaspoon salt

¾ teaspoon black pepper

⅓ cup packed chopped mixed fresh herbs, such as basil, chives, parsley, oregano, rosemary leaves, sage, tarragon and thyme

1. Preheat **Oster® Countertop Oven** to 450°F. Line oven tray with foil. Arrange potatoes and onion in prepared pan.

2. Combine oil, butter, garlic, salt and pepper in small bowl. Drizzle over potatoes and onion; toss well to coat.

3. Bake 30 minutes. Stir; bake 10 minutes. Add herbs; toss well. Continue baking 10 to 15 minutes or until vegetables are tender and browned.

Makes 6 servings

Sweet Potato Gratin

3 pounds sweet potatoes (about 5 large)

½ cup (1 stick) butter or margarine, divided

¼ cup plus 2 tablespoons packed light brown sugar, divided

2 eggs

⅔ cup orange juice

2 teaspoons ground cinnamon, divided

½ teaspoon salt

¼ teaspoon ground nutmeg

⅓ cup all-purpose flour

¼ cup uncooked old-fashioned oats

⅓ cup chopped pecans or walnuts

1. Preheat **Oster® Countertop Oven** to 350°F. Bake sweet potatoes about 1 hour or until tender. Or pierce sweet potatoes several times with fork and place on microwavable plate. Microwave on HIGH 16 to 18 minutes, rotating and turning potatoes over after 9 minutes. Let stand 5 minutes.

2. Cut hot sweet potatoes lengthwise into halves. Scrape hot pulp from skins into large bowl.

3. Beat ¼ cup butter and 2 tablespoons sugar into sweet potatoes with electric mixer at medium speed until butter is melted. Add eggs, orange juice, 1½ teaspoons cinnamon, salt and nutmeg. Beat until smooth. Pour mixture into 1½-quart baking dish or gratin dish; smooth top.

4. For topping, combine flour, oats, remaining ¼ cup sugar and remaining ½ teaspoon cinnamon in medium bowl. Cut in remaining ¼ cup butter until mixture resembles coarse crumbs. Stir in pecans. Sprinkle topping evenly over sweet potatoes.*

5. Bake 25 to 30 minutes or until sweet potatoes are heated through. For crisper topping, broil 5 inches from heat 2 to 3 minutes or until golden brown.

Makes 6 to 8 servings

At this point, Sweet Potato Gratin may be covered and refrigerated up to 1 day. Let stand at room temperature 1 hour before baking.

Mushroom Stuffing

2 cups mixed fresh mushrooms, trim any tough stems, chop roughly

½ cup yellow onion

2 cloves fresh garlic

1 tablespoon fresh rosemary

1 tablespoon fresh thyme

1 tablespoon butter

1 tablespoon olive oil

1 cup dry white wine or Madeira

1 rib celery, chopped

2 cups turkey or chicken broth

4 cups favorite bread for stuffing, cut into 1½-inch cubes

1. Preheat **Oster® Countertop Oven** to 350°F. Spray shallow 2-quart baking dish with nonstick cooking spray.

2. Add mushrooms, onion, garlic, rosemary and thyme to food processor. Pulse to finely mince.

3. Heat butter and oil in large saucepan over medium heat. Add mushroom mixture and cook, stirring frequently, about 5 minutes. Add wine and celery; continue cooking another 5 minutes. Add turkey broth and heat through. Turn off heat.

4. Place bread cubes in large bowl and pour mushroom mixture over them. Stir to moisten all bread. Spread stuffing evenly in baking dish.

5. Cover with foil. Bake 30 minutes, then uncover and bake additional 15 minutes to brown. Serve alongside turkey or chicken.

Makes 4 to 5 servings

Swiss-Style Twice Baked Potatoes

4 large evenly shaped baking potatoes (about 2½ pounds)

8 teaspoons butter or margarine, softened, divided

⅔ cup grated Emmentaler cheese*

⅔ cup grated Gruyère cheese*

½ teaspoon caraway seeds (optional)

4 teaspoons dry white wine

2 teaspoons kirsch (cherry brandy)

½ teaspoon minced garlic

½ teaspoon salt

*Emmentaler and Gruyère are imported Swiss cheeses that are aged longer than domestic Swiss. Any Swiss cheese can be used.

1. Preheat **Oster® Countertop Oven** to 425°F. Scrub potatoes. Dry well. Rub each potato with 1 teaspoon butter. Pierce potatoes several times with fork. Place in shallow baking dish at least 1 inch apart. Bake 50 to 60 minutes or until tender. Cool several minutes.

2. Meanwhile, place cheeses and caraway seeds, if desired, in small bowl. Toss well; set aside.

3. Cut off top one-third of potatoes. Scoop out potato pulp from bottom sections leaving ¼-inch shell. Place pulp in large bowl, reserving shells. Add pulp from potato tops to bowl; discard top skins.

4. Mash pulp until smooth. Add wine, kirsch, if desired, garlic, salt and remaining butter; mash to blend. Stir in cheese mixture; mash lightly or until all ingredients are well blended. Spoon mixture into potato shells, mounding evenly.

5. Place potatoes in baking dish. Bake 20 to 25 minutes or until tops are lightly browned and potatoes are heated through.

Makes 4 servings

Mediterranean Vegetables

¼ **cup marsala**

¼ **cup olive oil**

½ **teaspoon salt**

½ **teaspoon red pepper flakes**

2 **tablespoons chopped fresh thyme, plus extra for garnish**

3 **Italian eggplants**

1 **large zucchini, quartered**

6 **fresh baby artichokes, prepared (see Tip)**

½ **yellow pepper, sliced thin**

3 **fresh cherry peppers, cut in half**

4 **cloves garlic, cut in half**

4 or 5 **green and black olives**

1. Preheat **Oster® Countertop Oven** to highest heat setting. Combine marsala, olive oil, salt, pepper flakes and thyme in large bowl. Add eggplants, zucchini, artichokes and peppers; marinate 15 minutes. Remove vegetables from marinade and spread out evenly on roasting pan. Place pan in countertop oven and roast vegetables 15 to 20 minutes or until vegetables are tender.

2. Remove vegetables from oven and place on serving platter. Scatter olives around plate. Garnish with thyme, if desired.

Makes 2 to 3 servings

Tip: *Most baby artichokes have no fuzz or fibrous leaves in the center, the artichoke is completely edible once the outer leaves are trimmed off. Bend back the outer green leaves and snap them off at the base. Continue doing this until the leaves are half green (at the top) and half yellow. Using a stainless steel knife to minimize discoloration, cut off green top (green parts will be fibrous). Cut the stem level with the base and trim any remaining green from the base of the artichoke. Cut in half or quarter horizontally. If there are purple or pink leaves, cut them out (those leaves will be tough). If the interior is white the entire artichoke is edible. Place in acidulated water (water with a few drops of lemon juice). Place artichokes upright in a microwavable casserole. Heat, covered, in microwave 12 to 15 minutes. Cook until bases are tender when pierced with a fork and lower leaves pull away easily.*

main dishes

Chicken Wraps

½ **pound boneless, skinless chicken thighs**

½ **teaspoon Chinese 5-spice powder**

½ **cup canned bean sprouts, rinsed and drained**

2 **tablespoons minced green onion**

2 **tablespoons sliced almonds**

2 **tablespoons soy sauce**

4 **teaspoons hoisin sauce**

1 **to 2 teaspoons chili garlic sauce***

4 **large leaves romaine, iceberg or Bibb lettuce**

*Chili garlic sauce is available in the Asian foods section of most large supermarkets.

1. Preheat **Oster® Countertop Oven** to 350°F. Place chicken on oven tray; sprinkle with 5-spice powder. Bake 20 minutes or until chicken is cooked through. Cool.

2. Dice chicken. Place chicken, bean sprouts, green onion, almonds, soy sauce, hoisin sauce and chili garlic sauce in large bowl. Stir until blended. To serve, spoon ½ cup chicken mixture onto each lettuce leaf; roll or fold as desired.

Makes 4 servings

Aloha Sandwiches

2 boneless, skinless chicken breasts	**½ cup finely shredded red cabbage**
½ can (4 ounces) crushed pineapple, drained	**¼ cup grated carrot**
2 tablespoons mayonnaise	**¼ teaspoon vegetable oil**
¼ teaspoon garlic salt	**¼ sweet Maui onion, thinly sliced**
⅛ teaspoon salt	**4 slices Hawaiian-style sandwich bread**
⅛ teaspoon black pepper	**2 slices tomato**
½ teaspoon brown sugar	**½ mango, peeled and thinly sliced**

1. Pound chicken breast halves between 2 pieces of plastic wrap to ¼-inch thickness with flat side of meat mallet or rolling pin. Combine pineapple, mayonnaise, garlic salt, salt, pepper, and brown sugar in medium bowl; reserve 2 tablespoons marinade. Add chicken to remaining marinade, turning to coat well. Cover with plastic wrap; refrigerate at least 1 hour, turning chicken occasionally.

2. Preheat broiler in **Oster® Countertop Oven.** Coat broiler pan with nonstick cooking spray; place chicken in pan and brush with any remaining marinade. Broil 4 to 5 inches from heat, 5 to 6 minutes on each side or until no longer pink in center and internal temperature reaches 170°F.

3. Heat oil in medium skillet over medium heat. Add onion and cook 4 to 5 minutes or until caramelized, stirring often. In medium bowl, combine cabbage, carrot, onion and reserved ¼ cup marinade. Toast Hawaiian bread until lightly browned.

4. To assemble sandwiches, place 1 chicken breast, half of cabbage mixture, 1 tomato slice and half of mango slices between 2 pieces toasted bread. Repeat for remaining sandwich.

Makes 2 sandwiches

Stuffed Bell Pepper

½ cup chopped fresh tomatoes

1 teaspoon chopped fresh cilantro (optional)

½ clove garlic, minced

¼ teaspoon dried oregano

⅛ teaspoon ground cumin

4 ounces ground beef

¼ cup cooked brown or white rice

2 tablespoons cholesterol-free egg substitute or 1 egg white

1 tablespoon finely chopped onion

⅛ teaspoon salt

⅛ teaspoon black pepper

1 large bell pepper, any color, seeded and cut in half lengthwise

2 sheets (12 × 12 inches) heavy-duty foil, lightly sprayed with nonstick cooking spray

1. Preheat **Oster® Countertop Oven** to 400°F.

2. Combine tomatoes, cilantro, if desired, garlic, oregano and cumin in small bowl. Set aside.

3. Thoroughly combine beef, rice, egg substitute, onion, salt and black pepper in medium bowl. Stir ⅓ cup tomato mixture into beef mixture. Spoon filling evenly into pepper halves; place each pepper half on foil sheet.

4. Double fold sides and ends of foil to seal packet. Place on oven tray.

5. Bake 30 minutes or until beef is no longer pink and pepper halves are tender. Serve with remaining tomato salsa, if desired.

Makes 2 servings

Red Snapper Scampi

¼ cup (½ stick) butter or margarine, softened

1 tablespoon dry white wine

1½ teaspoons minced garlic

½ teaspoon grated lemon peel

⅛ teaspoon black pepper

1½ pounds red snapper, orange roughy or grouper fillets (4 to 5 ounces each)

1. Preheat **Oster® Countertop Oven** to 450°F. Combine butter, wine, garlic, lemon peel and pepper in small bowl until blended.

2. Place fish on foil-lined oven tray. Top with seasoned butter. Bake 10 to 12 minutes or until fish just begins to flake when tested with fork.

Makes 4 servings

Tip: *Serve fish with mixed salad greens, if desired. Or add sliced carrots, zucchini and bell pepper cut into matchstick-size strips to the tray with the fish for an easy vegetable side dish.*

Blue Corn Enchiladas with Crabmeat

3 tablespoons chopped onion

2 cloves garlic, minced

2 tablespoons butter or margarine

6 green chiles, roasted, peeled, stems and seeds removed, chopped

1 tablespoon red pepper flakes

2 tablespoons all-purpose flour

1 teaspoon ground cumin

1 cup dry white wine

1 cup heavy cream

½ cup sour cream

1 pound cooked lump crabmeat

2 cups Monterey Jack cheese, grated, divided

6 (8-inch) blue corn tortillas

6 green onions, green and white parts, chopped

Fresh cilantro, chopped (optional)

1. Cook and stir onion and garlic in butter until soft. Add green chiles. Stir in red pepper flakes, flour and cumin; heat 3 minutes.

2. Stir in wine and simmer until sauce thickens. Remove from heat; stir in heavy cream and sour cream.

3. Mix crabmeat in large bowl with 1 cup sauce and 1 cup cheese.

4. Preheat **Oster® Countertop Oven** to 350°F. Soften tortillas in damp towel in microwave, about 10 seconds. Coat 2-quart baking dish with nonstick cooking spray. Place 1 tortilla in dish, put several tablespoons crab mixture on tortilla and roll up, placing seam-side down in dish. Continue process with remaining tortillas and crab mixture.

5. Pour remaining sauce over tortillas; top with green onions and remaining cheese. Bake just long enough to heat through and melt cheese, about 15 minutes. Garnish with cilantro.

Makes 3 servings

Herb Caprese Sandwich

- **4 focaccia breads, cut into large squares**
- **4 beefsteak tomatoes (2 yellow and 2 red)**
- **16 ounces fresh buffalo mozzarella**
- **20 leaves fresh basil, plus extra for garnish**

- **1 tablespoon fresh rosemary, plus extra for garnish**
- **Black pepper**
- **1 teaspoon white wine vinegar**
- **4 teaspoons extra-virgin olive oil**
- **Black olives (optional)**

1. Warm or lightly toast focaccia breads in **Oster® Countertop Oven.** Place 1 focaccia bread on each serving plate.

2. Slice tomatoes to about ¼-inch thickness and arrange on top of bread, alternating red and yellow tomatoes. Slice mozzarella about same width and layer between tomatoes.

3. Place basil, rosemary, pepper, vinegar and olive oil in blender or food processor. Process until well blended. Drizzle over focaccia. Garnish with olives, fresh basil and rosemary.

Makes 4 servings

Chicken Parmesan

2 boneless, skinless chicken breasts

2 sheets (18 × 12 inches) heavy-duty foil, lightly sprayed with nonstick cooking spray

Salt and black pepper

1 cup pasta sauce

½ cup chopped onion

8 slices zucchini, quartered

¼ cup (1 ounce) shredded mozzarella cheese

2 tablespoons grated Parmesan cheese

Hot cooked spaghetti or linguini (optional)

1. Preheat **Oster® Countertop Oven** to 450°F.

2. Place 1 chicken breast in center of each sheet of foil. Season to taste with salt and pepper.

3. Combine pasta sauce, onion and zucchini. Pour half of sauce mixture over each chicken breast. Sprinkle with cheeses. Double fold sides and ends of foil to seal packets, leaving head space for heat circulation. Place packets on oven tray.

4. Bake 16 to 18 minutes until chicken is no longer pink in center. Remove from oven. Carefully open one end of each foil packet to allow steam to escape. Open packets and transfer contents to serving plates. Serve with spaghetti, if desired.

Makes 2 servings

Savory Stuffed Pork Chops

2 pork chops, cut 1½ inches thick

1½ cups seasoned bread cubes

1 cup dried sweetened cranberries

½ cup chopped celery

¼ cup chopped onion

1 egg, slightly beaten

3 tablespoons milk

2 tablespoons sliced almonds

2 tablespoons vegetable oil

2 teaspoons melted butter

1 tablespoon plus 1½ teaspoons minced fresh parsley, divided

¾ teaspoon salt

¼ teaspoon pepper

1 tablespoon chopped garlic

½ teaspoon red pepper flakes

¼ cup Calvados, cognac, brandy or apple juice

1. Preheat **Oster® Countertop Oven** to 350°F. With small paring knife, slice a pocket in rounded end of each pork chop.

2. Combine bread cubes, cranberries, celery, onion, egg, milk, almonds, oil, butter, 1½ teaspoons parsley, salt and pepper; mix well. Stuff each chop with mixture. Combine remaining 1 tablespoon parsley, garlic, red pepper and Calvados and brush or rub onto chops.

3. Bake on oven tray 1 hour or until instant read thermometer inserted into center of chops registers 160°F.

Makes 2 servings

Chicken Stuffed Peppers

2 pounds ground chicken

2 tablespoons chopped fresh
  parsley

4 cloves garlic, chopped

1 teaspoon chopped shallot

1 stalk fennel, diced

  Salt and black pepper

4 large bell peppers

1. Preheat **Oster® Countertop Oven** to 350°F. Combine chicken, parsley, garlic, shallot, fennel, salt and pepper in large bowl.

2. Remove tops from peppers and clean out seeds. Fill each pepper with chicken mixture. Bake 1 hour or until juices run clear.

Makes 4 servings

Lemon-Capered Pork Tenderloin

- 1 **boneless pork tenderloin (about ¾ pound)**
- ½ **tablespoon crushed capers**
- ½ **teaspoon dried rosemary, crushed**

- **Pinch black pepper**
- ½ **cup water**
- 2 **tablespoons lemon juice**

1. Preheat **Oster® Countertop Oven** to 350°F. Trim fat from tenderloin; discard. Set tenderloin aside.

2. Combine capers, rosemary and black pepper in small bowl. Rub mixture over tenderloin. Place tenderloin in shallow 2-quart baking dish. Pour water and lemon juice over tenderloin.

3. Bake, uncovered, about 20 minutes or until thermometer inserted into thickest part of tenderloin registers 160°F. Remove from oven; cover with foil. Allow to stand 10 minutes. Slice as desired and serve.

Makes 4 servings

Pecan Encrusted Turkey Breast

1 **boneless turkey breast (2 to 2½ pounds)**

1 **tablespoon olive oil**

1 **clove garlic, minced**

⅓ **cup chopped pecans**

⅓ **cup coarse bread crumbs**

1 **teaspoon grated orange peel**

¼ **teaspoon ground nutmeg**

¼ **cup jellied cranberry sauce**

Whole cranberry sauce and fresh fruit (optional)

1. Preheat **Oster® Countertop Oven** to 375°F. Remove skin from turkey breast. Cut off bones from bottom of breast so breast sits firmly on roasting rack. Place turkey on roasting rack. Brush oil over turkey and roast, uncovered, 30 minutes.

2. Mix garlic, pecans, bread crumbs, orange peel and nutmeg in small bowl.

3. Remove turkey from oven and brush surface with cranberry sauce. Press nut mixture on top of cranberry sauce, covering turkey evenly.

4. Return turkey to oven; bake 30 minutes or until meat thermometer reads 170°F. Remove from oven.

5. Let turkey stand 15 minutes before slicing. Garnish with whole cranberry sauce and fresh fruit, such as star fruit.

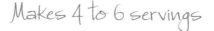

Makes 4 to 6 servings

Roasted Cornish Hens

6 thin slices pancetta or prosciutto

2 Cornish game hens, about ¾ pound each, at room temperature*

4 fresh sage leaves

2 bay leaves

2 sprigs rosemary

12 black olives (preferably small Gaeta or niçoise, pitted)

4 cloves of garlic, chopped

⅛ cup chopped fresh Italian parsley

2 teaspoons extra-virgin olive oil

Salt and black pepper

*While storing poultry at room temperature for a long period of time is unwise, it is an acceptable practice to allow refrigerated meats to come to room temperature before cooking. Place wrapped meat in a shallow dish or pie plate or rest in an unused sink for 10 or 15 minutes before cooking.

1. Preheat **Oster® Countertop Oven** to 400°F.

2. Tuck 3 slices pancetta inside each hen along with 2 sage leaves, bay leaf, sprig of rosemary and 6 olives. Mix together garlic, parsley and olive oil. Sprinkle salt and pepper all over outside of hens and rub into skin, rubbing with some of olive oil mixture at the same time. Set hens in shallow 2-quart baking dish. Sprinkle additional pancetta and herbs around dish, if desired.

3. Roast 45 minutes, then turn oven to 325°F and continue roasting 30 to 40 minutes longer or until hens are done and juices run clear when hens are pierced with fork. Serve immediately, with pan juices as sauce.

Makes 2 to 4 servings

Herbed Chicken and Vegetables

¾ teaspoon dried oregano, divided

1 teaspoon paprika

¼ teaspoon salt

⅛ teaspoon black pepper

2 skinless bone-in chicken breasts

2 sheets (18 × 12 inches each) heavy-duty foil, lightly sprayed with nonstick cooking spray

½ cup pasta sauce

4 cloves garlic, peeled and minced

½ medium green bell pepper, cut into squares

½ medium yellow bell pepper, cut into squares

½ cup chopped fresh mushrooms

¼ cup chopped onion

Parmesan cheese

Hot cooked egg noodles

1. Preheat **Oster® Countertop Oven** to 450°F. In small bowl, combine ½ teaspoon oregano, paprika, salt and pepper; mix well.

2. Place each chicken breast on a foil sheet. Sprinkle each chicken breast with half of oregano mixture. Combine pasta sauce, garlic, bell peppers, mushrooms, onion and remaining ¼ teaspoon oregano in medium bowl. Pour half of sauce mixture over each chicken breast.

3. Double foil sides and ends of foil to seal packets, leaving head space for heat circulation. Place packets on oven tray.

4. Bake 23 to 25 minutes or until chicken juices run clear. Carefully open ends of packets to allow steam to escape. Open packets and transfer contents to serving plates. Sprinkle with Parmesan cheese. Serve with noodles.

Makes 2 servings

Quick Tip: *Love the taste of garlic but can't stand the odor? Cooking in foil helps contain food smells until time it's to serve.*

Phyllo Tart of Mushrooms, Potatoes and Spinach with Mushroom Jus

5 pounds assorted mushrooms (domestic, cremini, shiitake, oyster, hedgehog, chanterelle and hen of the woods)

1 cup clarified butter, divided

10 shallots, peeled and diced (reserve scraps for Mushroom Jus)

¼ bunch fresh thyme, picked and chopped (reserve stems for Mushroom Jus)

¼ bunch fresh Italian parsley, picked, washed and chopped (reserve stems for Mushroom Jus)

2 pounds Yukon Gold potatoes, scrubbed clean

6 tablespoons butter, divided

Salt and black pepper

4 bunches spinach, washed and stems removed

12 sheets phyllo dough

¼ bunch fresh thyme, picked and chopped

Mushroom Jus (recipe follows)

1. Clean and slice mushrooms. Reserve stems. Cook and stir each type of mushroom separately in clarified butter until golden brown (use ½ cup clarified butter total). Add some shallots toward end of cooking time for each batch, and cook until soft. Mix mushrooms together; add thyme and parsley.

2. Preheat **Oster® Countertop Oven** to 350°F. Rub potatoes with 4 tablespoons butter; add salt and pepper. Place on oven tray and roast 20 to 30 minutes or until cooked through. Slice.

3. Meanwhile, melt 2 tablespoons butter in large skillet; add spinach and cook. Season with salt and pepper. Drain well and cool.

4. Cut sheets of phyllo dough into quarters and keep covered with damp towel. Arrange into 8 stacks, each containing 3 quarter-sheets of phyllo, brushing each sheet with clarified butter and sprinkling with thyme, salt and pepper.

5. Place 3 slices potato, one-fourth spinach and one-fourth cooked mushrooms on each of 4 stacks of phyllo. Top with remaining 4 stacks, butter side down. Roll up all edges and seal.

6. Bake on oven tray 10 minutes or until golden brown. Drizzle tarts with Mushroom Jus.

Makes 4 servings

Mushroom Jus

Heat 2 tablespoons butter in small saucepan; sauté reserved mushroom stems, shallot scraps and herb stems until golden. Add 2 cups chicken broth and reduce by half. Pour through fine mesh strainer, discard solids and return to saucepan. Add 2 more tablespoons butter, ¼ bunch chopped fresh Italian parsley and salt and black pepper to taste.

Herbed Rack of Lamb

4 cloves garlic

4 large fresh basil leaves

¼ cup chopped fresh parsley

¼ teaspoon each red, white and black pepper

2 racks of spring lamb, about 7 chops each

1 large onion, peeled and sliced into rings

1. Place garlic, basil, parsley and peppers in food processor and pulse until coarsely ground. Set aside.

2. Preheat **Oster® Countertop Oven** to 350°F. Lay racks of lamb on oven tray with roasting rack with bones facing each other. Push racks as close together as possible. Rub herb mixture all over lamb. Toss onion with remaining herb mixture and place on rack between lamb racks.

3. Roast 15 minutes per pound or until quick-read thermometer reads 140°F for rare.

Makes 6 servings

Apple-Cranberry Turnovers

Filling
- 1 small Granny Smith apple, peeled and diced (about ½ cup)
- 1 tablespoon dried cranberries
- 1 tablespoon packed dark brown sugar
- ½ tablespoon butter
- ½ tablespoon bourbon (optional)
- ⅛ teaspoon ground cinnamon
- Pinch ground allspice
- ½ sheet puff pastry dough, thawed

Topping
- 1 teaspoon granulated sugar
- ⅛ teaspoon ground cinnamon
- ½ tablespoon butter, melted

1. Place filling ingredients in medium saucepan. Cook and stir 2 to 3 minutes over medium heat until apples start to soften. Remove from heat and cool completely.

2. Unfold pastry sheet onto lightly floured surface. Cut dough into 2 squares. Brush edges with water. Spoon ¼ cup apple mixture in center of each square and fold dough to create a triangle. Seal edges by pinching seams with fork. Line oven tray with parchment paper. Place turnovers on tray. Cover and refrigerate 30 minutes to relax dough.

3. Preheat **Oster® Countertop Oven** to 400°F. Make small slash on top of each turnover to release steam. Bake 15 to 20 minutes or until puffed and golden brown.

4. For topping, combine granulated sugar and cinnamon. Brush equal amounts of butter on each warm turnover and sprinkle with cinnamon sugar. Serve warm or at room temperature.

Makes 2 turnovers

Open-Faced Pear and Walnut Breakfast Sandwiches

1 **pear, peeled, cored and chopped**	⅛ **teaspoon ground nutmeg**
¼ **cup unsweetened applesauce**	2 **slices multigrain bread**
1½ **tablespoons chopped walnuts**	2 **tablespoons plus 2 teaspoons finely shredded Swiss cheese**
1 **tablespoon sugar**	**Chopped dried cranberries**
¼ **teaspoon ground cinnamon**	

1. Preheat **Oster® Countertop Oven** to 400°F. Spray oven tray with nonstick cooking spray. Combine pears, applesauce, walnuts, sugar, cinnamon and nutmeg in small bowl.

2. Toast bread; top evenly with pear mixture. Place on baking tray. Top each sandwich evenly with Swiss cheese. Bake 8 minutes or until cheese melts.

3. Garnish with cranberries.

Makes 2 servings

Biscuit and Sausage Bake

2 cups biscuit baking mix

½ cup milk

1 egg

1 teaspoon vanilla

1 cup fresh or frozen blueberries, thawed if frozen

6 fully cooked breakfast sausage links, thawed if frozen

Maple syrup, warmed

1. Preheat **Oster® Countertop Oven** to 350°F. Spray 8-inch square baking dish with nonstick cooking spray. Whisk baking mix, milk, egg and vanilla in medium bowl. Fold in blueberries. (Batter will be stiff.) Spread batter in prepared pan.

2. Cut each sausage link into small pieces; sprinkle over batter. Bake 22 minutes or until lightly browned on top. Cut into squares; serve with maple syrup.

Makes 6 servings

Honey Granola with Yogurt

½ **cup uncooked old-fashioned oats**

¼ **cup sliced almonds**

2 **tablespoons toasted wheat germ**

1 **tablespoon orange juice**

1 **tablespoon honey**

½ **teaspoon ground cinnamon**

1½ **cups whole strawberries**

4 **containers (6 ounces each) plain fat-free yogurt**

1 **teaspoon vanilla**

1. Preheat **Oster® Countertop Oven** to 325°F. Lightly spray 8-inch square baking pan with nonstick cooking spray; set aside.

2. Combine oats, almonds and wheat germ in small bowl. Combine orange juice, honey and cinnamon in another small bowl. Add juice mixture to oat mixture; mix well. Spread mixture evenly in prepared pan. Bake 20 to 25 minutes or until toasted, stirring twice during baking. Transfer mixture to large sheet of foil to cool completely.

3. Cut 3 strawberries in half for garnish. Slice remaining strawberries. Combine yogurt and vanilla in medium bowl. Layer yogurt mixture, granola and sliced strawberries in 6 dessert dishes. Garnish with strawberry halves.

Makes 6 servings

Oatmeal Brûlée with Raspberry Sauce

Brûlée

- 4 cups water
- ½ teaspoon salt
- 3 cups old-fashioned oats
- 1 cup whipping cream
- ½ teaspoon vanilla
- ¼ cup granulated sugar
- 3 egg yolks
- 3 tablespoons brown sugar

Raspberry Sauce

- 6 ounces frozen sweetened raspberries
- ½ cup granulated sugar
- ¼ cup water
- 1 teaspoon orange extract

1. For brûlée: Preheat **Oster® Countertop Oven** to 300°F. Line oven tray with foil. In medium saucepan, heat 4 cups water and salt over high heat. When water simmers, add oats and reduce heat to low. Cook, stirring occasionally, 3 to 5 minutes or until water is absorbed and oats are tender. Divide oatmeal among 4 large ramekins or ovenproof bowls. Place on prepared oven tray; set aside.

2. In separate medium saucepan, scald cream over high heat; do not boil. Remove from heat; stir in vanilla. In small bowl, mix ¼ cup granulated sugar and egg yolks with fork or whisk. Pour about ½ cup scalded cream in a thin stream into egg mixture, stirring quickly; stir egg mixture into saucepan of scalded cream, whisking until well blended and smooth. Ladle cream mixture equally over oatmeal in ramekins. Bake 35 minutes or until nearly set. Remove from oven; preheat broiler.

3. Meanwhile, purée raspberries, ½ cup granulated sugar, water and orange extract in blender or food processor. Pour sauce through strainer to remove seeds; discard seeds.

4. Sprinkle 1½ teaspoons brown sugar evenly over each brûlée. Broil 3 to 5 minutes or until tops are caramelized. Cool 5 to 10 minutes before serving. Serve with raspberry sauce.

Makes 4 servings

Note: *This brûlée has the texture of rice pudding and the taste of sweet custard, with a crème brûlée-like topping. Brûlée (broo-LAY) comes from the French word for "burned."*

Blueberry-Orange French Toast Casserole

6 slices 100% whole wheat bread, cut into 1-inch pieces

1 cup fresh (not frozen) blueberries

½ cup sugar

½ cup fat-free (skim) milk

2 eggs

4 egg whites

1 tablespoon grated orange peel

½ teaspoon vanilla

1. Preheat **Oster® Countertop Oven** to 350°F. Coat 8-inch square baking dish with nonstick cooking spray. Place bread and blueberries in dish; toss gently to combine.

2. Whisk sugar into milk in medium bowl until dissolved. Whisk in eggs, egg whites, orange peel and vanilla; pour over bread mixlure. Toss to coat. Let stand 5 minutes.

3. Bake 40 to 45 minutes or until top of bread is browned and center is almost set. Let stand 5 minutes before serving.

Makes 6 servings

Bacon & Egg Cups

6 slices bacon, cut into thirds

3 eggs or ¾ cup egg substitute

¼ cup half-and-half

¼ cup diced bell peppers (red, green or a combination)

¼ cup shredded pepper-Jack cheese

⅛ teaspoon salt

⅛ teaspoon black pepper

1. Preheat **Oster® Countertop Oven** to 350°F. Lightly spray 6-cup standard (2½-inch) muffin pan with nonstick cooking spray.

2. Arrange bacon slices flat in single layer on plate lined with paper towel. Do not overlap. Top with additional sheets of paper towel and microwave on HIGH 2 to 3 minutes or until cooked yet pliable. Place 3 bacon slices in each cup, overlapping 1 inch in bottom of cup.

3. Beat eggs, half-and-half, bell peppers, cheese, salt and pepper in medium bowl until well blended. Fill each cup with ¼ cup egg mixture. Bake 20 to 25 minutes or until eggs are set in center. Run knife around edge of each cup before removing from pan.

Makes 6 servings

Tip: *To save prep time, look for mixed diced bell peppers in the produce section of the grocery store.*

Crunchy French Toast Sticks

2 (1-inch) slices Italian bread
1⅓ cups corn flakes cereal, crushed
1 egg, slightly beaten
¼ cup skim milk
⅓ tablespoon sugar
⅓ teaspoon vanilla

⅓ teaspoon ground cinnamon
Pinch ground nutmeg
¼ cup vanilla low-fat yogurt
4 teaspoons maple syrup
Ground cinnamon (optional)

1. Preheat **Oster® Countertop Oven** to 375°F. Lightly spray oven tray with nonstick cooking spray; set aside. Remove crusts from bread, if desired. Cut each bread slice into 3 strips. Place cereal on waxed paper; set aside.

2. Stir egg, milk, sugar, vanilla, cinnamon and nutmeg in shallow bowl. Dip bread strips in egg mixture, turning to generously coat all sides. Roll in cereal, coating all sides. Place on prepared baking tray.

3. Bake 20 to 25 minutes or until golden brown, turning once after 15 minutes.

4. Meanwhile, combine yogurt and syrup in small bowl. Sprinkle with additional cinnamon, if desired. Serve French toast sticks with yogurt mixture for dipping.

Makes 2 servings

Ooey-Gooey Pineapple Buns

⅔ **cup packed brown sugar**

¼ **cup maple syrup**

2 **tablespoons butter, melted**

1 **teaspoon vanilla**

1 **can (8 ounces) pineapple tidbits, drained**

½ **cup chopped pecans**

½ **cup flaked coconut**

1 **package (12 ounces) refrigerated flaky biscuits (10 biscuits)**

1. Preheat **Oster® Countertop Oven** to 350°F.

2. Combine brown sugar, maple syrup, butter and vanilla in 9-inch square baking dish. Sprinkle with pineapple tidbits, pecans and coconut.

3. Cut biscuits into quarters; arrange over coconut. Bake 25 to 30 minutes or until deep golden brown. Invert onto serving plate; serve warm.

Makes 10 servings

Feta Brunch Bake

1 medium red bell pepper	**⅓ cup chopped onion**
2 bags (10 ounces each) fresh spinach, stemmed	**2 tablespoons chopped fresh parsley**
6 eggs	**¼ teaspoon dried dill weed**
6 ounces crumbled feta cheese	**Dash black pepper**

1. Preheat broiler in **Oster® Countertop Oven.** Place bell pepper on foil-lined oven tray. Broil 15 to 20 minutes or until blackened on all sides, turning every 5 minutes with tongs. Place in paper bag; close bag and set aside to cool about 15 to 20 minutes. To peel pepper, cut around core, twist and remove. Cut in half and rub off skin; rinse under cold water. Cut into ½-inch pieces.

2. Place 1 quart water in 2-quart saucepan over high heat; bring to a boil. Add spinach. Return to a boil; boil 2 to 3 minutes or until crisp-tender. Drain; immediately plunge spinach into cold water. Drain; let stand until cool enough to handle. Squeeze spinach to remove excess water; finely chop.

3. Preheat oven to 400°F. Grease 1-quart baking dish. Beat eggs in large bowl with electric mixer at medium speed until foamy. Stir in spinach, bell pepper, cheese, onion, parsley, dill and black pepper. Pour egg mixture into prepared dish. Bake 20 minutes or until set. Let stand 5 minutes before serving. Garnish as desired.

Makes 4 servings

Ham and Cheese Bread Pudding

- 1 small loaf (8 ounces) sourdough, country French or Italian bread, cut into 1-inch-thick slices
- 3 tablespoons butter or margarine, softened
- 8 ounces ham or smoked ham, cubed
- 2 cups (8 ounces) shredded mild or sharp Cheddar cheese
- 3 eggs
- 2 cups milk
- 1 teaspoon dry mustard
- ½ teaspoon salt
- ⅛ teaspoon white pepper

1. Preheat **Oster® Countertop Oven** to 350°F. Grease 2-quart baking dish. Spread 1 side of each bread slice with butter. Cut into 1-inch cubes; place on bottom of prepared dish. Top with ham; sprinkle with cheese.

2. Beat eggs in medium bowl. Whisk in milk, mustard, salt and pepper. Pour egg mixture evenly over bread mixture. Cover; refrigerate at least 6 hours or overnight.

3. Bake bread pudding, uncovered, 45 to 50 minutes or until puffed and golden brown and knife inserted into center comes out clean. Garnish as desired. Serve immediately.

Makes 8 servings

French Toast Kabobs

8 slices French bread (each about 1 inch thick, 2½ to 3 inches in diameter)

1 cup milk

2 eggs, lightly beaten

3 tablespoons granulated sugar

2 teaspoons vanilla

⅛ teaspoon salt

¾ cup tangerine juice or orange juice

¼ cup honey

2 teaspoons cornstarch

¼ teaspoon ground ginger or ground cinnamon

Powdered sugar

1 cup fresh raspberries

1. Preheat broiler in **Oster® Countertop Oven.** Generously coat broiling rack and oven tray with nonstick cooking spray. Soak 4 (12-inch) wooden skewers in water while preparing bread.

2. Cut each bread slice in half. Beat milk, eggs, granulated sugar, vanilla and salt in shallow dish until well blended. Place bread pieces in egg mixture. Let stand 5 minutes, turning to soak all sides.

3. Meanwhile, combine tangerine juice, honey, cornstarch and ginger in small saucepan; bring to a boil over medium-high heat, stirring constantly. Cook and stir 1 minute more. Set aside and keep warm.

4. Thread bread pieces on prepared skewers. Place on prepared rack of broiler pan. Broil 5 to 7 minutes or until lightly browned. Turn skewers; broil 3 to 5 minutes more or until lightly browned.

5. Spoon juice mixture onto 4 plates; top with French toast skewer. Sprinkle with powdered sugar and raspberries. Serve immediately.

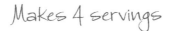

Makes 4 servings

Hash Brown Breakfast Casserole

3 cups frozen shredded hash brown potatoes

1½ cups (6 ounces) finely chopped extra-lean ham

¾ cup (3 ounces) shredded reduced-fat Cheddar cheese

¼ cup sliced green onions

1 can (12 ounces) evaporated fat-free milk

1 tablespoon all-purpose flour

1 cup cholesterol-free egg substitute

½ teaspoon black pepper

1. Preheat **Oster® Countertop Oven** to 350°F. Lightly coat 8-inch square baking dish with nonstick cooking spray.

2. Layer potatoes, ham, cheese and onions in dish. Gradually whisk milk into flour in small bowl. Stir in egg substitute and pepper. Pour over all. Cover and refrigerate 4 to 24 hours.

3. Bake, uncovered, 55 to 60 minutes or until knife inserted into center comes out clean. Remove from oven; let stand 10 minutes before serving.

Makes 6 servings

Hawaiian Breakfast Pizza

2 teaspoons barbecue sauce or
pineapple jam

1 English muffin, split in half and
toasted

1 slice (1 ounce) smoked ham,
diced

½ cup pineapple chunks

2 tablespoons shredded Cheddar
cheese

1. Spread barbecue sauce over each muffin half; place on foil-lined oven tray. Sprinkle ham and pineapple chunks over muffin halves; top with cheese.

2. Toast in **Oster® Countertop Oven** about 2 minutes or until cheese is melted.

Makes 1 serving

muffins & quick breads

Quick Chocolate Chip Sticky Buns

2 tablespoons butter

1 package (11 ounces) refrigerated French bread dough

¼ cup sugar

1 teaspoon ground cinnamon

½ cup mini semisweet chocolate chips

⅓ cup pecan pieces, toasted

1 tablespoon maple syrup

1. Preheat **Oster® Countertop Oven** to 350°F. Place butter in 9-inch round cake pan; place pan in oven while preheating to melt butter.

2. Meanwhile, unroll dough on cutting board or clean work surface. Combine sugar and cinnamon in small bowl; sprinkle evenly over dough. Top with chocolate chips. Starting with short side, roll up dough and filling jelly-roll style. Cut into 8 slices with serrated knife.

3. Remove pan from oven. Stir pecans and maple syrup into melted butter; mix well. Arrange slices cut-side down in pan, pressing gently into nut mixture.

4. Bake 20 to 22 minutes or until golden brown. Immediately invert pan onto serving plate. Scrape any nuts or butter mixture remaining in pan onto tops of buns. Serve warm.

Makes 8 sticky buns

Black Forest Banana Bread

1 jar (10 ounces) maraschino cherries

1¾ cups all-purpose flour

2 teaspoons baking powder

½ teaspoon salt

⅔ cup packed brown sugar

⅓ cup butter, softened

1 cup mashed ripe bananas (about 2 large)

2 eggs

1 cup semisweet chocolate chips

¾ cup chopped pecans

1. Preheat **Oster® Countertop Oven** to 350°F. Lightly spray 9 × 5-inch loaf pan with nonstick cooking spray. Drain cherries, reserving 2 tablespoons juice. Coarsely chop cherries.

2. Combine flour, baking powder and salt in medium bowl. Beat brown sugar and butter in large bowl with electric mixer until creamy. Beat in bananas, eggs and reserved cherry juice until well blended. Stir in flour mixture, chopped cherries, chocolate chips and pecans just until blended. Pour into prepared pan.

3. Bake 1 hour or until golden brown and toothpick inserted into center comes out clean. Cool in pan on wire rack 10 minutes. Remove bread from pan; cool completely on wire rack.

Makes 1 loaf

Lemon-Cardamom Scones with Lemon Drizzle

1¼ cups all-purpose flour	¼ teaspoon salt
¾ cup oat bran	¼ cup (½ stick) cold butter
2 tablespoons granulated sugar	1 egg, lightly beaten
2 teaspoons grated lemon peel, divided	1 container (6 ounces) lemon low-fat yogurt
2 teaspoons baking powder	3 tablespoons powdered sugar
¾ teaspoon ground cardamom	2 teaspoons lemon juice
¼ teaspoon baking soda	

1. Preheat **Oster® Countertop Oven** to 400°F. Lightly coat oven tray with nonstick cooking spray; set aside.

2. Combine flour, oat bran, granulated sugar, 1½ teaspoons lemon peel, baking powder, cardamom, baking soda and salt in large bowl. Cut in butter with pastry blender or 2 knives until mixture is crumbly.

3. Stir together egg and yogurt in small bowl until blended. Stir into flour mixture just until moistened. On lightly floured surface gently knead dough 10 to 12 times. Pat dough into 7½-inch circle. Cut into 8 wedges. Place wedges 2 inches apart on prepared baking tray.

4. Bake 11 to 13 minutes or until scones are golden brown. Remove from baking tray to wire rack. Cool 10 minutes. Stir together powdered sugar, lemon juice and remaining ½ teaspoon lemon peel until smooth; drizzle over scones.

Makes 8 servings

Lemon-Ginger Scones: Substitute ground ginger for ground cardamom.

Maple Magic Muffins

½ cup plus 3 tablespoons maple syrup,* divided

¼ cup chopped walnuts

2 tablespoons butter, melted

2 cups all-purpose flour

¾ cup sugar

2 teaspoons baking powder

½ teaspoon baking soda

½ teaspoon salt

¼ teaspoon ground cinnamon

¾ cup plus 1 tablespoon milk

½ cup vegetable oil

1 egg

½ teaspoon vanilla

*For best flavor and texture, use pure maple syrup, not pancake syrup.

1. Preheat **Oster® Countertop Oven** to 400°F. Grease all 12 cups of 2 standard (2½-inch) 6-muffin muffin tins. Place 2 teaspoons maple syrup, 1 teaspoon walnuts and ½ teaspoon melted butter in each cup.

2. Combine flour, sugar, baking powder, baking soda, salt and cinnamon in large bowl; mix well.

3. Whisk milk, oil, egg, remaining 3 tablespoons maple syrup and vanilla in medium bowl until well blended. Add to flour mixture; stir just until blended. Spoon batter into prepared muffin cups, filling two-thirds full. Place 1 muffin tin on oven tray to catch any drips (maple syrup may overflow slightly); set second tin aside.

4. Bake 20 to 25 minutes or until toothpick inserted into centers comes out clean; bake second pan of muffins. Invert pan of completed muffins onto wire rack covered with waxed paper. Cool muffins slightly; serve warm.

Makes 12 muffins

Mustard Beer Biscuits

2 cups all-purpose flour

2 teaspoons baking powder

¾ teaspoon salt

¼ cup cold shortening

¼ cup (½ stick) cold butter

½ cup beer

1 tablespoon plus 1 teaspoon prepared mustard, divided

1 tablespoon milk

1. Preheat **Oster® Countertop Oven** to 425°F. In large bowl, combine flour, baking powder and salt. Cut in shortening and butter until mixture resembles coarse crumbs. Combine beer and 1 tablespoon mustard; stir into crumb mixture just until blended. Turn onto floured surface; knead gently 8 times.

2. Pat dough to ½-inch thickness. Cut out biscuits with 2-inch round biscuit cutter. Reroll scraps and cut out additional biscuits. Place 1 inch apart on greased oven tray. Combine remaining mustard with milk and brush over tops. Bake 13 to 15 minutes or until lightly browned.

Makes about 1 dozen biscuits

Peach Pecan Upside-Down Pancake

2 tablespoons butter, melted

2 tablespoons packed light brown sugar

1 tablespoon maple syrup

½ (16-ounce) package frozen unsweetened peach slices, thawed

3 tablespoons pecan pieces

⅔ cup biscuit baking mix

2 eggs

⅓ cup fat-free (skim) milk

½ teaspoon vanilla

Additional maple syrup (optional)

1. Preheat **Oster® Countertop Oven** to 400°F. Spray 8- or 9-inch pie pan with nonstick cooking spray.

2. Pour butter into pie pan. Sprinkle with brown sugar and maple syrup. Arrange peach slices in single layer on top in decorative circle. Sprinkle with pecans; set aside.

3. Place baking mix in medium bowl. Whisk together eggs, milk and vanilla in small bowl; stir into baking mix just until dry ingredients are moistened. Pour batter over peaches. Bake 15 to 18 minutes or until lightly browned and firm to the touch. Remove from oven. Let cool 1 minute. Run knife around outer edge. Invert pancake onto serving plate. Serve immediately with additional maple syrup, if desired.

Makes 6 servings

Pumpkin Bread for One

⅓ cup all-purpose flour

2 tablespoons granulated sugar

1 tablespoon packed brown sugar

1 tablespoon currants

1 teaspoon baking powder

½ teaspoon pumpkin pie spice or ground cinnamon

⅛ teaspoon salt

3 tablespoons canned solid-pack pumpkin

1 egg

1 tablespoon vegetable oil

¼ cup powdered sugar

1 teaspoon lemon juice or water

1. Preheat **Oster® Countertop Oven** to 350°F. Coat inside of ovenproof 12-ounce coffee mug with nonstick cooking spray.

2. Mix flour, sugars, currants, baking powder, pumpkin pie spice and salt in small bowl. Stir pumpkin, egg and oil into dry ingredients in bowl; stir until well blended. Pour into prepared mug.

3. Bake 30 minutes or until toothpick inserted into center comes out clean. Mix powdered sugar and lemon juice in small food storage bag; seal and knead until blended. Cut small corner from bag; drizzle glaze over bread.

Makes 1 serving

Chili Corn Bread

Nonstick cooking spray
¼ cup chopped red bell pepper
¼ cup chopped green bell pepper
2 small jalapeño peppers,* minced
2 cloves garlic, minced
¾ cup corn
1½ cups yellow cornmeal
½ cup all-purpose flour
2 tablespoons sugar
2 teaspoons baking powder

½ teaspoon baking soda
½ teaspoon ground cumin
½ teaspoon salt
1½ cups low-fat buttermilk
1 egg
2 egg whites
4 tablespoons butter, melted

*Jalapeño peppers can sting and irritate the skin, so wear rubber gloves when handling peppers and do not touch your eyes.

1. Preheat **Oster® Countertop Oven** to 425°F. Spray 8-inch square baking pan with cooking spray; set aside.

2. Spray small skillet with cooking spray. Add bell peppers, jalapeños and garlic; cook and stir 3 to 4 minutes or until peppers are tender. Stir in corn; cook 1 to 2 minutes. Remove from heat.

3. Combine cornmeal, flour, sugar, baking powder, baking soda, cumin and salt in large bowl. Add buttermilk, egg, egg whites and butter; mix until blended. Stir in corn mixture. Pour batter into prepared baking pan.

4. Bake 25 to 30 minutes or until golden brown. Cool on wire rack. Cut into 12 squares before serving.

Makes 12 servings

Carrot Quick Bread

2 cups finely shredded carrots

¾ cup vegetable oil

½ cup granulated sugar

½ cup packed brown sugar

1 teaspoon baking soda

2 eggs, lightly beaten

1½ cups all-purpose flour

½ cup whole wheat flour

2 teaspoons baking powder

1 teaspoon ground cinnamon

½ teaspoon salt

½ teaspoon ground nutmeg

¾ cup chopped walnuts

1. Preheat **Oster® Countertop Oven** to 350°F. Grease 9 × 5-inch loaf pan.

2. Combine carrots, oil, sugars and baking soda in large bowl; stir until well blended. Add eggs; stir until well blended. Combine flours, baking powder, cinnamon, salt and nutmeg in medium bowl until blended; stir into carrot mixture. Stir in walnuts. Pour batter into prepared pan; let stand 5 minutes.

3. Bake 50 to 60 minutes or until toothpick inserted into center comes out clean. Cool on wire rack. Wrap in foil or plastic wrap; let stand at room temperature overnight before slicing.

Makes 1 loaf

Sweet Potato Muffins

½ cup all-purpose flour

3 tablespoons chopped walnuts

3 tablespoons golden raisins

2 tablespoons packed brown sugar

1 teaspoon baking powder

¼ teaspoon ground cinnamon

⅛ teaspoon salt

⅛ teaspoon baking soda

Pinch ground nutmeg

¼ cup mashed cooked sweet potato

3 tablespoons milk

2 tablespoons butter, melted

1 egg, beaten

½ teaspoon vanilla

1. Preheat **Oster® Countertop Oven** to 400°F. Grease 6 standard (2½-inch) muffin cups.

2. Combine flour, walnuts, raisins, brown sugar, baking powder, cinnamon, salt, baking soda and nutmeg in medium bowl; stir until well blended. Combine sweet potato, milk, butter, egg and vanilla in large bowl; stir until well blended. Add flour mixture to sweet potato mixture; stir just until dry ingredients are moistened. Spoon batter evenly into prepared muffin cups.

3. Bake 15 minutes or until toothpick inserted into centers comes out clean. Cool in pans 5 minutes; remove to wire racks to cool.

Makes 6 muffins

Blueberry Hill Bread

2 cups all-purpose flour

¾ cup packed brown sugar

2 teaspoons baking powder

1 teaspoon baking soda

1 teaspoon salt

½ teaspoon ground nutmeg

1 egg

¾ cup buttermilk or sour milk

3 tablespoons vegetable oil or melted butter

1 cup fresh or thawed frozen blueberries

1. Preheat **Oster® Countertop Oven** to 350°F. Fit food processor with steel blade. Measure flour, sugar, baking powder, baking soda, salt and nutmeg into work bowl. Process 5 seconds to mix. Combine egg, buttermilk and oil; pour over flour mixture. Process just until flour is moistened, 5 to 10 seconds. Do not overprocess. Batter should be lumpy.

2. Sprinkle blueberries over batter. Pulse on/off just to mix blueberries into batter. (Batter will be stiff.) Turn into greased 8½ × 4½ × 2½-inch loaf pan. Bake until toothpick inserted into center comes out clean, 50 to 60 minutes. Cool bread 15 minutes in pan. Remove from pan and cool on wire rack.

Makes 1 loaf

Ultimate White and Dark Chocolate Cookies

2⅓ cups all-purpose flour

1 teaspoon baking soda

¼ teaspoon salt

1 cup (2 sticks) butter, softened

¾ cup granulated sugar

¾ cup packed brown sugar

2 eggs

2 tablespoons almond-flavored liqueur or water

1 teaspoon vanilla

1½ cups white chocolate chips

1½ cups bittersweet or semisweet chocolate chips

1 cup coarsely chopped pecans

1. Preheat **Oster® Countertop Oven** to 375°F. Cut several pieces of parchment paper to fit oven tray.

2. Combine flour, baking soda and salt in medium bowl.

3. Beat butter and sugars in large bowl with electric mixer until smooth and creamy. Beat in eggs, liqueur and vanilla. Add flour mixture; beat until well blended. Stir in chocolate chips and pecans. Drop dough by teaspoonfuls 2 inches apart onto parchment-lined oven tray.

4. Bake 8 to 10 minutes or until firm in center. Do not overbake. Remove on parchment paper to wire racks to cool. Repeat with remaining dough.

Makes about 5 dozen cookies

Tip: *After stirring in chocolate chips and pecans, dough may be refrigerated in an airtight container for up to 1 week. Refrigerated dough may take slightly longer to bake.*

Aztec Brownies

½ **cup (1 stick) butter, softened**
1 **cup semisweet chocolate chips**
1 **egg**
1 **egg yolk**
½ **cup sugar**
1½ **teaspoons instant coffee granules or powder**

1½ **teaspoons vanilla**
6 **tablespoons all-purpose flour**
1 **teaspoon baking powder**
½ **teaspoon ground cinnamon**
½ **to 1 teaspoon chili powder**
¼ **teaspoon salt**
6 **tablespoons sliced almonds**

1. Preheat **Oster® Countertop Oven** to 350°F. Spray 8-inch square baking pan with nonstick cooking spray. Line pan with foil and spray foil.

2. Place butter and chocolate chips in medium microwavable bowl; microwave on HIGH 30 seconds. Stir until mixture is smooth. (If lumps remain, microwave 10 seconds more and stir again.)

3. Whisk eggs, sugar, coffee granules and vanilla in medium bowl until well blended. Stir in warm chocolate mixture; set aside to cool 10 minutes. Whisk flour, baking powder, cinnamon, chili powder and salt in large bowl; stir in chocolate mixture until well blended. Pour into prepared pan.

4. Bake 15 minutes; remove pan from oven and sprinkle with almonds. Bake 20 minutes longer or until top is no longer shiny and toothpick inserted into center comes out almost clean. Do not overbake. Cool completely in pan on wire rack before cutting into squares or triangles.

Makes 9 to 12 brownies

Tip: *For easier cutting, refrigerate the brownies a few hours before cutting.*

Cranberry Coconut Bars

Filling

- ½ **cup fresh or frozen cranberries**
- ½ **cup dried sweetened cranberries**
- ⅓ **cup granulated sugar**
- 2 **tablespoons water**
- **Grated peel of ½ lemon**

Crust

- ½ **cup plus 2 tablespoons all-purpose flour**
- 6 **tablespoons uncooked old-fashioned oats**
- ¼ **teaspoon baking soda**
- ¼ **teaspoon salt**
- 6 **tablespoons unsalted butter, softened**
- ½ **cup firmly packed light brown sugar**
- ½ **cup chopped toasted pecans***
- ½ **cup shredded sweetened coconut**

*To toast pecans, spread in single layer on oven tray. Bake in preheated 350°F oven 5 to 7 minutes or until golden brown, stirring frequently.

1. Preheat **Oster® Countertop Oven** to 400°F. Grease and flour 8-inch square baking pan.

2. For filling, combine fresh cranberries, dried cranberries, granulated sugar, water and lemon peel in medium saucepan. Cook, stirring frequently, 10 to 15 minutes over medium-high heat until mixture is pulpy. Mash cranberries with back of spoon. Cool to lukewarm.

3. For crust, combine flour, oats, baking soda and salt in medium bowl. Beat butter and brown sugar in large bowl with electric mixer at medium speed until creamy. Add flour mixture; beat just until blended. Stir in pecans and coconut. Reserve ¾ cup; pat remaining crumb mixture in bottom of prepared pan. Bake 10 minutes; remove from oven.

4. Gently spread cranberry filling evenly over crust. Sprinkle with reserved crumb mixture. Bake 18 to 20 minutes or until bars are set and crust is golden brown. Cool completely before cutting into bars.

Makes 8 to 12 bars

Note: *You can make these bars when fresh or frozen cranberries aren't available. Prepare the filling using 1 cup dried sweetened cranberries, ½ cup water and peel of ½ lemon; cook 8 to 10 minutes over medium heat, stirring frequently. Use as directed in step 4.*

Intense Mint-Chocolate Brownies

Brownies

- 1 cup (2 sticks) butter
- 4 squares (1 ounce each) unsweetened chocolate
- 1½ cups granulated sugar
- 3 eggs
- ½ teaspoon salt
- ½ teaspoon mint extract
- ½ teaspoon vanilla
- ¾ cup all-purpose flour

Mint Frosting

- 6 tablespoons butter, softened
- 1 teaspoon mint extract
- 2 to 3 drops green food coloring
- 2 cups powdered sugar
- 2 to 3 tablespoons milk

Chocolate Glaze

- ⅓ cup semisweet chocolate chips
- 2 tablespoons butter

1. Preheat **Oster® Countertop Oven** to 325°F. Grease and flour 9-inch square baking pan.

2. For brownies, melt butter and chocolate in top of double boiler over simmering water. Beat chocolate mixture, granulated sugar, eggs, salt, mint extract and vanilla in large bowl until well blended. Stir in flour. Spread batter in prepared pan. Bake 35 minutes or until top is firm and edges begin to pull away from sides of pan. Cool completely in pan on wire rack.

3. For mint frosting, beat butter, mint extract and food coloring in large bowl with electric mixer at medium speed until fluffy. Add powdered sugar, ½ cup at a time, beating well after each addition. Beat in milk, 1 tablespoon at a time, until spreading consistency is reached. Spread frosting over cooled brownies.

4. For chocolate glaze, place chocolate chips and butter in microwavable bowl. Microwave on LOW (30%) 1 minute; stir. Repeat until chocolate is melted and mixture is smooth. Drizzle glaze over frosting. Let stand 30 minutes or until glaze is set. Cut into bars.

Makes 2 dozen brownies

Peanut Butter & Banana Cookies

¼ **cup (½ stick) butter**

½ **cup mashed ripe banana**

½ **cup natural peanut butter**

¼ **cup thawed frozen unsweetened apple juice concentrate**

1 **egg**

1 **teaspoon vanilla**

1 **cup all-purpose flour**

½ **teaspoon baking soda**

¼ **teaspoon salt**

½ **cup chopped salted peanuts**

Whole salted peanuts (optional)

1. Preheat **Oster® Countertop Oven** to 375°F. Line oven tray with parchment paper.

2. Beat butter in large bowl until creamy. Add banana and peanut butter; beat until smooth. Blend in apple juice concentrate, egg and vanilla. Beat in flour, baking soda and salt. Stir in chopped peanuts.

3. Drop 6 rounded tablespoonfuls of dough 2 inches apart onto prepared tray; top each with one whole peanut, if desired. Bake 8 minutes or until set. Transfer on parchment paper to wire rack and cool completely. Line oven tray with new sheet of parchment and repeat using all remaining dough. Store in tightly covered container.

Makes 2 dozen cookies

Chocolate Coconut Almond Macaroons

1⅓ cups flaked sweetened coconut (3½ -ounce can)

⅔ cup sugar

2 egg whites

½ teaspoon vanilla

¼ teaspoon almond extract

Pinch salt

4 ounces sliced almonds, coarsely crushed

20 whole almonds

Chocolate Ganache (recipe follows)

1. Combine coconut, sugar, egg whites, vanilla, almond extract and salt in medium bowl; mix well. Fold in sliced almonds. Cover and refrigerate at least 1 hour or overnight.

2. Preheat **Oster® Countertop Oven** to 350°F. Line oven tray with parchment paper. Roll scant tablespoonfuls dough into balls. Place 1 inch apart on prepared tray. Press almond on top of each cookie. Bake 15 minutes or until light brown. Cool cookies on pan 5 minutes. Transfer to wire rack; cool completely.

3. Meanwhile, prepare Chocolate Ganache. Let ganache cool 10 to 15 minutes.

4. Dip bottom of each cookie into ganache. Place cookies onto clean parchment or waxed paper-lined baking sheet Refrigerate until ganache is firm. Store covered in refrigerator.

Makes about 20 cookies

Chocolate Ganache

½ cup whipping cream

1 tablespoon butter

1 cup semisweet or bittersweet chocolate chips

Heat whipping cream and butter in medium saucepan until just hot (do not boil). Remove from heat; add chocolate chips and let stand 1 minute. Stir until smooth. Keep warm (ganache is semifirm at room temperature). Refrigerate leftover ganache.

Makes 2 cups ganache

Mocha Cream Cheese Mousse Brownies

Brownie

- 1 **package (19½ ounces) brownie mix**
- ½ **cup vegetable oil**
- 2 **eggs**
- ¼ **cup water**
- 1½ **tablespoons instant coffee granules, divided**

Mousse Topping

- 1 **package (4 ounces) cream cheese, softened**
- 1 **cup powdered sugar**
- ¼ **cup unsweetened cocoa powder**
- 1 **teaspoon vanilla**
- 1 **container (8 ounces) frozen whipped topping, thawed**
- ½ **recipe Chocolate Ganache (see recipe page 130), optional**

1. Preheat **Oster® Countertop Oven** to 350°F. Spray 2 (8-inch) square pans with nonstick cooking spray.

2. Combine brownie mix, oil, eggs, water and 1½ teaspoons coffee granules in medium bowl. Mix according to package directions. Divide brownie batter between prepared pans. Bake pans one at a time 26 to 28 minutes or until toothpick inserted 1 inch from edge comes out clean. Transfer to wire rack; cool completely.

3. Meanwhile, mix cream cheese, powdered sugar, cocoa powder, vanilla and remaining coffee granules in medium bowl until smooth. Fold in whipped topping. Cover with plastic wrap; refrigerate until needed.

4. Spread mousse topping evenly over brownies. Prepare ganache, if desired. Pour warm ganache into medium food storage bag; seal bag. Cut small hole from one corner. Pipe lines of ganache over mousse. Drag toothpick or paring knife through ganache to create a design, if desired. Refrigerate until well-chilled. Cut into bars. Store covered in refrigerator.

Makes 2 dozen brownies

Chocolate Chip Shortbread

¼ **cup (½ stick) butter, softened**

¼ **cup sugar**

½ **teaspoon vanilla**

½ **cup all-purpose flour**

⅛ **teaspoon salt**

¼ **cup mini semisweet chocolate chips**

1. Preheat **Oster® Countertop Oven** to 375°F.

2. Beat butter and sugar in large bowl with electric mixer at medium speed until light and fluffy. Beat in vanilla. Add flour and salt; beat at low speed. Stir in chocolate chips.

3. Press dough into ungreased 8-inch round cake pan.

4. Bake in oven 12 minutes or until edges are golden brown. Score shortbread into 8 triangles with sharp knife, taking care not to cut completely through shortbread.

5. Cool in pans on wire racks 10 minutes. Invert shortbread onto wire racks; cool completely. Break into triangles.

Makes 8 cookies

Chocolate Pinwheels

2 cups (4 sticks) unsalted butter, softened

1 cup powdered sugar

¼ cup packed light brown sugar

½ teaspoon salt

4 cups all-purpose flour

½ cup semisweet chocolate chips, melted

1 tablespoon unsweetened cocoa

1. Beat butter, powdered sugar, brown sugar and salt in large bowl with electric mixer at medium speed 2 minutes or until light and fluffy. Gradually add flour; beat well after each addition. Divide dough in half; set one half aside. Add melted chocolate and cocoa to remaining dough; beat until well blended.

2. Shape chocolate and plain doughs into 4 balls each. Roll 1 ball plain dough into 12×6-inch rectangle on lightly floured surface; transfer to sheet of parchment paper or plastic wrap. Roll 1 ball chocolate dough into 12×6-inch rectangle on lightly floured surface; place over plain dough. Tightly roll up jelly-roll style, starting at wide end, to form 12-inch log. If dough crumbles or breaks, press back together and continue to roll (effect will be marbled, not spiralled, but just as attractive). Wrap in plastic wrap; refrigerate 1 hour. Repeat with remaining dough.

3. Preheat **Oster® Countertop Oven** to 300°F. Cut each log into 20 slices; place on ungreased oven tray. Bake 13 to 15 minutes or until cookies are set and lightly browned. Cool 5 minutes on tray. Remove to wire racks to cool completely.

Makes 80 cookies

Tip: Once shaped into 12-inch log, dough may be refrigerated in an airtight container for up to 1 week before slicing and baking. Refrigerated dough may take slightly longer to bake.

Lemon Melts

¼ **cup powdered sugar**
¼ **cup packed light brown sugar**
¼ **cup canola oil**
¼ **cup (½ stick) butter, melted**
1½ **teaspoons lemon juice**

1½ **teaspoons vanilla**
½ **teaspoon almond extract**
1 **cup all-purpose flour**
¼ **teaspoon cream of tartar**
¼ **teaspoon baking soda**

1. Preheat **Oster® Countertop Oven** to 350°F. Grease oven tray.

2. Beat sugars, oil, butter, lemon juice, vanilla and almond extract in large bowl with electric mixer at medium speed until smooth.

3. Combine flour, cream of tartar and baking soda in separate large bowl; gradually beat into butter mixture until stiff dough forms.

4. Drop dough by rounded tablespoonfuls 2 inches apart onto prepared tray; flatten slightly with fork. Bake 20 minutes or until edges are lightly browned. Cool 1 minute on tray. Remove to wire racks; cool completely.

Makes about 2 dozen cookies

Pumpkin Oatmeal Cookies

1 cup all-purpose flour

1 teaspoon ground cinnamon

½ teaspoon salt

½ teaspoon ground nutmeg

¼ teaspoon baking soda

1½ cups packed light brown sugar

½ cup (1 stick) butter, softened

1 egg

1 teaspoon vanilla

½ cup solid-pack pumpkin

2 cups uncooked old-fashioned oats

1 cup dried cranberries (optional)

1. Preheat **Oster® Countertop Oven** to 350°F. Line oven tray with parchment paper.

2. Sift flour, cinnamon, salt, nutmeg and baking soda into medium bowl. Beat brown sugar and butter in large bowl with electric mixer at medium speed about 5 minutes or until light and fluffy.

3. Beat in egg and vanilla. Add pumpkin; beat at low speed until blended. Beat in flour mixture just until blended. Add oats; mix well. Stir in cranberries, if desired. Drop dough by rounded tablespoonfuls 2 inches apart onto prepared tray.

4. Bake 12 minutes or until golden brown. Cool 1 minute on baking tray. Remove to wire racks; cool completely. Repeat with remaining dough.

Makes about 2 dozen cookies

cakes, pies & tarts

Cherry-Almond Streusel Cake

Cake
- 1½ cups biscuit baking mix
- ½ cup milk
- 2 tablespoons granulated sugar
- 2 tablespoons vegetable oil
- 2 eggs
- 1 teaspoon vanilla
- ¼ teaspoon almond extract
- ½ to ¾ cup dried cherries*

Topping
- ½ cup slivered almonds
- ½ cup quick oats
- ⅓ cup biscuit baking mix
- ⅓ cup packed dark brown sugar
- ¼ teaspoon ground cinnamon
- 3 tablespoons cold butter, cubed

*Substitute an equivalent quantity of your favorite dried fruit, such as dried cranberries or raisins.

1. Preheat **Oster® Countertop Oven** to 350°F. Spray 8-inch round baking pan with nonstick cooking spray.

2. Combine all cake ingredients, except cherries, in medium bowl. Stir until well blended. Gently stir in cherries. Spread batter into prepared pan; set aside.

3. Combine all topping ingredients, except butter, in medium bowl. Cut in butter with pastry blender or 2 knives until butter is the size of peas.

4. Sprinkle topping evenly over batter. Bake 20 to 25 minutes or until toothpick inserted into middle of cake comes out almost clean. Let stand at least 30 minutes before serving.

Makes 12 servings

Blueberry Yogurt Cake

1 cup applesauce
½ cup granulated sugar
¼ cup (½ stick) butter, softened
2 eggs
1 teaspoon vanilla
1½ cups cake flour
1 teaspoon baking powder

¼ teaspoon baking soda
½ cup plain or vanilla yogurt
1 cup fresh blueberries
1 teaspoon all-purpose flour
1 cup chopped walnuts
½ cup packed brown sugar
1 teaspoon ground cinnamon

1. Preheat **Oster® Countertop Oven** to 350°F. Line 8-inch square baking pan with foil and spray with nonstick cooking spray.

2. Beat applesauce, granulated sugar and butter in medium bowl with electric mixer at medium speed 2 minutes. Beat in eggs and vanilla. Sift cake flour, baking powder and baking soda into small bowl. Add to applesauce mixture with yogurt; beat until smooth. Toss berries with all-purpose flour and gently fold into batter.

3. Combine walnuts, brown sugar and cinnamon in small bowl. Sprinkle half of walnut mixture over bottom of prepared pan. Pour half of batter over walnut mixture. Repeat layers.

4. Bake 30 to 35 minutes or until toothpick inserted into center comes out clean. Cool completely on wire rack. Invert cake onto serving plate. Garnish as desired.

Makes 9 servings

Crunch Peach Cobbler

⅓ cup plus 1 tablespoon granulated sugar, divided

1 tablespoon cornstarch

1 can (29 ounces) or 2 cans (16 ounces each) cling peach slices in syrup, drained reserving ¾ cup syrup

½ teaspoon vanilla

2 cups all-purpose flour, divided

½ cup packed light brown sugar

⅓ cup uncooked old-fashioned or quick oats

¼ cup (½ stick) butter, melted

½ teaspoon ground cinnamon

½ teaspoon salt

½ cup shortening

4 to 5 tablespoons cold water

Whipped cream (optional)

1. Combine ⅓ cup granulated sugar and cornstarch in small saucepan. Slowly add reserved peach syrup. Stir well. Add vanilla. Cook over low heat, stirring constantly, until thickened. Set aside.

2. For crumb topping, combine ½ cup flour, brown sugar, oats, butter and cinnamon in small bowl; stir until mixture forms coarse crumbs. Set aside.

3. Preheat **Oster® Countertop Oven** to 325°F. Combine remaining 1½ cups flour, remaining 1 tablespoon granulated sugar and salt in small bowl. Cut in shortening with pastry blender or 2 knives until mixture forms pea-sized pieces. Sprinkle water, 1 tablespoon at a time, over flour mixture. Toss lightly with fork until mixture holds together. Press together to form ball.

4. Roll dough into 10-inch square, ⅛ inch thick. Fold dough in half, then in half again. Carefully place folded dough in center of 8-inch square baking dish. Unfold and press onto bottom and about 1 inch up sides of dish. Arrange peaches over crust. Pour peach sauce over peaches. Sprinkle with reserved crumb topping.

5. Bake 50 to 60 minutes. Serve warm or at room temperature. Garnish with whipped cream.

Makes about 6 servings

Mixed Berry Crisp

2 teaspoons plus 1 tablespoon granulated sugar, divided

1 tablespoon cornstarch*

2 cups mixed berries (thawed if frozen)

½ cup old-fashioned oats

¼ cup packed brown sugar

2 tablespoons all-purpose flour

½ teaspoon ground cinnamon

⅛ teaspoon ground ginger

⅛ teaspoon salt

3 tablespoons cold butter

Vanilla ice cream (optional)

*Increase to 2 tablespoons if using frozen berries.

1. Preheat **Oster® Countertop Oven** to 375°F.

2. Combine 2 teaspoons granulated sugar and cornstarch in medium bowl. Add berries; toss to coat evenly. Divide berry mixture between 2 (5-inch) heart-shaped pie plates or other 5-inch baking dishes.

3. Combine oats, brown sugar, flour, remaining 1 tablespoon granulated sugar, cinnamon, ginger and salt in small bowl. Cut in butter using pastry blender or 2 knives, then mix with fork until mixture resembles coarse crumbs. Sprinkle topping evenly over berries. Bake 20 to 25 minutes or until topping is golden brown and berries are bubbling around edges. Serve warm with vanilla ice cream, if desired.

Makes 2 servings

Topsy-Turvy Banana Crunch Cake

⅓ cup uncooked old-fashioned oats

3 tablespoons packed brown sugar

1 tablespoon all-purpose flour

¼ teaspoon ground cinnamon

2 tablespoons butter

2 tablespoons chopped pecans

1 package (9 ounces) yellow cake mix without pudding in mix

½ cup sour cream

½ cup mashed banana (about 1 medium banana)

1 egg, slightly beaten

1. Preheat **Oster® Countertop Oven** to 350°F. Lightly grease 8-inch square baking pan.

2. Combine oats, brown sugar, flour and cinnamon in small bowl. Cut in butter with pastry blender or 2 knives until crumbly. Stir in pecans. Set aside.

3. Beat cake mix, sour cream, banana and egg in medium bowl with electric mixer at low speed about 1 minute or until blended. Beat at medium speed 1 to 2 minutes or until smooth. Spoon half of batter into prepared pan; sprinkle with half of oat mixture. Top with remaining batter and topping.

4. Bake 25 to 30 minutes or until toothpick inserted into center comes out clean. Cool completely in pan on wire rack.

Makes 9 servings

Apple Crunch Pie

- **1 refrigerated pie crust**
- **1¼ cups all-purpose flour, divided**
- **1 cup granulated sugar**
- **6 tablespoons (¾ stick) melted butter, divided**
- **1½ teaspoons ground cinnamon, divided**
- **¾ teaspoon ground nutmeg, divided**
- **½ teaspoon ground ginger**
- **¼ teaspoon salt**
- **4 cups diced peeled apples**
- **½ cup packed brown sugar**
- **½ cup chopped walnuts**

1. Preheat **Oster® Countertop Oven** to 350°F. Place dough in 9-inch pie pan; flute edge as desired.

2. Combine ¼ cup flour, granulated sugar, 2 tablespoons melted butter, 1 teaspoon cinnamon, ½ teaspoon nutmeg, ginger and salt in large bowl; mix well. Add apples; toss to coat. Place apple mixture in crust.

3. Combine remaining 1 cup flour, remaining 4 tablespoons melted butter, ½ teaspoon cinnamon, ¼ teaspoon nutmeg, brown sugar and walnuts in small bowl. Sprinkle evenly over apple mixture.

4. Bake 45 to 55 minutes or until apples are tender.

Makes 8 servings

Baked Pear Dessert

⅓ **cup unsweetened apple cider or apple juice, divided**

2 **tablespoons dried cranberries or raisins**

1 **tablespoon toasted sliced almonds**

⅛ **teaspoon ground cinnamon**

1 **medium unpeeled pear (about 6 ounces), cut in half lengthwise and cored**

½ **cup vanilla ice cream or frozen yogurt**

1. Preheat **Oster® Countertop Oven** to 350°F. Combine 1 teaspoon cider, cranberries, almonds and cinnamon in small bowl.

2. Place pear halves, cut sides up, in baking dish. Evenly mound almond mixture on top of pear halves. Pour remaining cider into dish. Cover with foil.

3. Bake pear halves 35 to 40 minutes or until pears are soft, spooning cider in dish over pears once or twice during baking. Serve warm with ice cream.

 Makes 2 servings

Mini Strawberry Shortcakes

Strawberry Filling
- ½ **cup fresh strawberries, sliced**
- 1 **teaspoon granulated sugar, or more to taste**

Shortcakes
- ¼ **cup plus 3 tablespoons all-purpose flour**
- 2 **teaspoons granulated sugar**
- ¼ **tablespoon baking powder**

Pinch salt
- 2 **tablespoons plus 2 teaspoons fat-free (skim) milk**
- 1 **tablespoon vegetable oil**

Topping
- ¼ **cup vanilla yogurt**
- ¾ **tablespoon packed light brown sugar**
- **Fresh mint leaves (optional)**

Strawberry Filling

Combine strawberries and granulated sugar in medium bowl. Refrigerate until ready to use.

Shortcakes

1. Preheat **Oster® Countertop Oven** to 400°F. Line oven tray with foil.

2. Combine flour, granulated sugar, baking powder and salt in medium bowl. Combine milk and oil in small bowl; add to flour mixture. Stir with fork until mixture forms rough dough.

3. Turn dough out onto floured work surface. Divide in half. Quickly shape each half into disk ½ inch thick.

4. Place biscuits on ungreased oven tray. Bake 12 to 15 minutes or until golden brown. Remove pan from oven; cool completely on wire rack.

Topping

1. Combine yogurt and brown sugar in medium bowl. Stir until smooth.

2. Split biscuits in half horizontally. Place half strawberry filling on bottom layer of each biscuit. Cover with biscuit tops. Drizzle topping over shortcakes. Garnish with any remaining strawberries and mint leaves.

Makes 2 servings

White Chocolate Cranberry Tart

1 refrigerated pie crust

1 cup sugar

2 eggs

¼ cup (½ stick) butter, melted

2 teaspoons vanilla

½ cup all-purpose flour

6 squares (1 ounce each) white chocolate, chopped

½ cup chopped macadamia nuts, lightly toasted*

½ cup dried cranberries, coarsely chopped

*Toast chopped macadamia nuts in hot skillet over medium heat about 3 minutes or until fragrant.

1. Preheat **Oster® Countertop Oven** to 350°F. Place pie crust in 9-inch tart pan with removable bottom or pie pan.

2. Combine sugar, eggs, butter and vanilla in large bowl; mix well. Stir in flour until well blended. Add white chocolate, nuts and cranberries.

3. Pour filling into unbaked crust. Bake 50 to 55 minutes or until top of tart is crusty and deep golden brown and knife inserted into center comes out clean.

4. Cool completely on wire rack.

Makes 8 servings

Serve it with Style!: Top each serving with a dollop of whipped cream flavored with ground cinnamon, a favorite liqueur and grated orange peel.

Wild Berry Cobbler with Lavender and Vanilla Ice Cream

1 tablespoon cornstarch	Juice of 3 lemons
2 cups sugar, divided	1 cup butter, softened
½ cup water	1 cup all-purpose flour
2 cups strawberries, stemmed and quartered	1½ teaspoons baking powder
2 cups blueberries	½ teaspoon salt
2 cups blackberries	1 cup buttermilk
2 cups raspberries	1 tablespoon lavender
	Vanilla ice cream (optional)

1. Combine cornstarch and 1 cup sugar in saucepan with ½ cup water; heat over medium heat. Allow mixture to come to a boil and thicken.

2. Pour mixture into large bowl with berries and lemon juice. Gently mix and place in shallow 2-quart baking dish.

3. Preheat **Oster® Countertop Oven** to 375°F.

4. Combine remaining 1 cup sugar and butter in food processor. Process until consistency is like sand. Add flour, baking powder, salt, buttermilk and lavender. Pulse until ingredients are well mixed. (It will not come together like dough.)

5. Top berries with flour mixture and bake 45 minutes or until golden. Serve hot topped with vanilla ice cream.

Makes 6 servings

Warm Financier Cakes with Seasonal Berries

3 tablespoons ground almonds or almond flour (meal)

3½ cups powdered sugar, sifted

¾ cup all-purpose flour, plus some for molds

5 egg whites

1½ cups melted butter, plus some for molds

½ teaspoon almond extract

3 tablespoons granulated sugar

2 pints assorted berries, cleaned (slice strawberries)

1. Preheat **Oster® Countertop Oven** to 400°F.

2. Mix ground almonds, powdered sugar and flour.

3. In separate bowl, beat egg whites with electric mixer until they are stiff.

4. Stir melted butter and almond extract into dry ingredients. Fold in egg whites.

5. Spread batter into 8 individual cake molds or ramekins and bake 7 to 10 minutes (longer if molds are deep), or until golden around edges.

6. Mix sugar and berries and let sit about 20 minutes.

7. To serve, place warm financier cake on each plate and serve with berries.

Makes 8 servings

index

A

Aegean Feta Bruschetta.................12
Aloha Sandwiches 64
Apple and Cheese Pockets 16
Apple Crunch Pie.........................148
Apple-Cranberry Turnovers.............82
Apricot BBQ Glazed Shrimp
    and Bacon 21
Aztec Brownies 122

B

Bacon & Egg Cups 94
Baked Pear Dessert.......................150
Baked Risotto with Asparagus,
    Spinach & Parmesan 38
Bar Cookies
    Chocolate Chip Shortbread 134
    Cranberry Coconut Bars 124
Beef
    Home-Style Shepherd's Pie 30
    Midweek Moussaka 28
    No-Chop Pastitsio 26
    Stuffed Bell Pepper......................65
Biscuit and Sausage Bake..............86
Black Forest Banana Bread 104
Blue Corn Enchiladas with
    Crabmeat....................................68
Blueberry Hill Bread 119
Blueberry Yogurt Cake 140
Blueberry-Orange French Toast
    Casserole.....................................92
Brownies
    Aztec Brownies...........................122
    Intense Mint-Chocolate
        Brownies 126
    Mocha Cream Cheese Mousse
        Brownies 132

C

Cakes
    Blueberry Yogurt Cake...............140
    Cherry-Almond Streusel
        Cake...138
    Mini Strawberry Shortcakes 152
    Topsy-Turvy Banana
        Crunch Cake......................146
    Warm Financier Cakes with
        Seasonal Berries 155
Carrie's Sweet Potato Casserole ...39
Carrot Quick Bread........................117
Cherry-Almond Streusel Cake 138
Chicken
    Aloha Sandwiches 64
    Chicken Parmesan.......................70
    Chicken Stuffed Peppers.............73
    Chicken Wraps 62
    Coconut Chicken Tenders with
        Spicy Mango Salsa 18
    Curried Chicken Pot Pies.............41
    Glazed Bacon-Wrapped
        Chicken....................................10
    Green Chile-Chicken
        Casserole 42
    Herbed Chicken and
        Vegetables 78
    Roasted Cornish Hens.................77
    Shrimp and Chicken Paella 32
Chicken Parmesan 70
Chicken Stuffed Peppers 73
Chicken Wraps 62
Chile-Corn Quiche.........................40
Chili Corn Bread 116
Chocolate Chip Shortbread.........134
Chocolate Coconut Almond
    Macaroons 130

Chocolate Pinwheels 135

Coconut Chicken Tenders with
   Spicy Mango Salsa.......................18

Cookies

   Chocolate Coconut Almond
      Macaroons 130

   Chocolate Pinwheels.................135

   Lemon Melts...............................136

   Peanut Butter & Banana
      Cookies 128

   Pumpkin Oatmeal Cookies 137

   Ultimate White and Dark
      Chocolate Cookies 120

Corn Pudding 48

Cranberry Coconut Bars 124

Crunch Peach Cobbler 142

Crunchy French Toast Sticks 95

Curried Chicken Pot Pies................41

D

Desserts

   Apple Crunch Pie.......................148

   Baked Pear Dessert 150

   Crunch Peach Cobbler 142

   Mixed Berry Crisp 144

   White Chocolate
      Cranberry Tart 153

   Wild Berry Cobbler with
      Lavender and Vanilla Ice
      Cream 154

F

Festive Corn Casserole....................34

Feta Brunch Bake............................97

French Toast Kabobs 99

G

Glazed Bacon-Wrapped Chicken.10

Green Chile-Chicken Casserole 42

H

Ham and Cheese Bread
   Pudding 98

Hash Brown Breakfast
   Casserole.....................................100

Hawaiian Breakfast Pizza 101

Herb Caprese Sandwich.................69

Herbed Chicken and
   Vegetables 78

Herbed Rack of Lamb.....................81

Home-Style Shepherd's Pie.............30

Honey Granola with Yogurt 88

I

Intense Mint-Chocolate
   Brownies.......................................126

L

Lemon Melts 136

Lemon-Capered Pork
   Tenderloin 74

Lemon-Cardamom Scones with
   Lemon Drizzle 106

M

Maple Magic Muffins....................108

Mediterranean Roasted Tomatoes 54

Mediterranean Vegetables 61

Midweek Moussaka 28

Mini Strawberry Shortcakes...........152

Mixed Berry Crisp............................144

Mocha Cream Cheese Mousse
   Brownies.......................................132

Mushroom Stuffing 59

Mustard Beer Biscuits 110

N

No-Chop Pastitsio.............................26

O

Oatmeal Brûlée with Raspberry
   Sauce..90

index

Ooey-Gooey Pineapple Buns 96

Open-Faced Pear and Walnut
  Breakfast Sandwiches 84

Oven "Fries" 56

Oven-Roasted Asparagus 44

Oven-Roasted Potatoes and
  Onions with Herbs 57

P

Peach Pecan Upside-Down
  Pancake 112

Peanut Butter &
  Banana Cookies 128

Pecan Encrusted Turkey Breast 76

Phyllo Tart of Mushrooms,
  Potatoes and Spinach
  with Mushroom Jus 80

Poblano Pepper Kabobs 52

Pork

  Apricot BBQ Glazed Shrimp
    and Bacon 21

  Bacon & Egg Cups 94

  Bacon-Wrapped
    BBQ Chicken 10

  Biscuit and Sausage Bake 86

  Ham and Cheese
    Bread Pudding 98

  Hash Brown Breakfast
    Casserole 100

  Hawaiian Breakfast Pizza 101

  Home-Style Shepherd's Pie 30

  Lemon-Capered Pork
    Tenderloin 74

  Roasted Cornish Hens 77

  Savory Stuffed Pork Chops 72

  Zucchini Pizza Bites 8

Pumpkin Bread for One 114

Pumpkin Oatmeal Cookies 137

Q

Quick Chocolate Chip
  Sticky Buns 102

R

Red Snapper Scampi 66

Roasted Cornish Hens 77

S

Salmon Wontons with Ginger
  Soy Sauce 22

Sausage-Stuffed Mushrooms 14

Savory Stuffed Pork Chops 72

Seafood

  Apricot BBQ Glazed Shrimp
    and Bacon 21

  Blue Corn Enchiladas with
    Crabmeat 68

  Red Snapper Scampi 66

  Salmon Wontons with Ginger
    Soy Sauce 22

  Shrimp and Chicken Paella 32

  Spiced Halibut, Pineapple and
    Pepper Skewers 20

Sesame-Honey Vegetable
  Casserole 24

Shrimp and Chicken Paella 32

Sides

  Baked Risotto with Asparagus,
    Spinach & Parmesan 38

  Carrie's Sweet Potato
    Casserole 39

  Corn Pudding 48

  Festive Corn Casserole 34

  Mediterranean Roasted
    Tomatoes 54

  Mediterranean Vegetables 61

  Mushroom Stuffing 59

  Oven "Fries" 56

  Oven-Roasted Asparagus 44

  Oven-Roasted Potatoes and
    Onions with Herbs 57

  Poblano Pepper Kabobs 52

  Sesame-Honey Vegetable
    Casserole 24

  Sweet Potato Gratin 58

Swiss-Style Twice Baked
Potatoes......................................60

Tricolored Pepper Salad..............50

Veggies and Couscous................46

Zucchini Tomato Bake 36

Spiced Halibut, Pineapple and
Pepper Skewers 20

Spicy Glazed Pecans........................6

Stuffed Bell Pepper 65

Sweet & Savory Brie in
Puff Pastry 23

Sweet Potato Gratin 58

Sweet Potato Muffins......................118

Swiss-Style Twice
Baked Potatoes 60

T

Topsy-Turvy Banana
Crunch Cake 146

Tricolored Pepper Salad..................50

Triple-Pepper Tomato Provolone
Lasagna..43

Turkey

Pecan Encrusted Turkey Breast...76

Poblano Pepper Kabobs.............52

Sausage-Stuffed Mushrooms.......14

U

Ultimate White and Dark
Chocolate Cookies....................120

V

Vegetarian

Aegean Feta Bruschetta.............12

Apple and Cheese Pockets........16

Apple-Cranberry Turnovers 82

Blueberry-Orange French Toast
Casserole 92

Carrie's Sweet Potato
Casserole 39

Chile-Corn Quiche 40

Corn Pudding................................48

Crunchy French Toast Sticks........95

Festive Corn Casserole 34

Feta Brunch Bake ....,...............97

French Toast Kabobs....................99

Herb Caprese Sandwich 69

Honey Granola with Yogurt.........88

Mediterranean Roast
Tomatoes 54

Mediterranean Vegetables.........61

Oatmeal Brûlée with
Raspberry Sauce.......................90

Ooey-Gooey Pineapple Buns.....96

Open-Faced Pear and Walnut
Breakfast Sandwich 84

Oven "Fries" 56

Oven-Roasted Asparagus...........44

Oven-Roasted Potatoes and
Onions with Herbs 57

Sesame-Honey Vegetable
Casserole 24

Sweet & Savory Brie in
Puff Pastry 23

Spicy Glazed Pecans....................6

Sweet Potato Gratin 58

Swiss-Style Twice
Baked Potatoes.........................60

Tricolored Pepper Salad 50

Triple-Pepper Tomato
Provolone Lasagna...................43

Zucchini Tomato Bake 36

Veggies and Couscous 46

W

Warm Financier Cakes with
Seasonal Berries 155

White Chocolate
Cranberry Tart 153

Wild Berry Cobbler with
Lavender and Vanilla
Ice Cream 154

Z

Zucchini Pizza Bites...........................8

Zucchini Tomato Bake 36

metric conversion chart

VOLUME MEASUREMENTS (dry)

$1/8$ teaspoon = 0.5 mL
$1/4$ teaspoon = 1 mL
$1/2$ teaspoon = 2 mL
$3/4$ teaspoon = 4 mL
1 teaspoon = 5 mL
1 tablespoon = 15 mL
2 tablespoons = 30 mL
$1/4$ cup = 60 mL
$1/3$ cup = 75 mL
$1/2$ cup = 125 mL
$2/3$ cup = 150 mL
$3/4$ cup = 175 mL
1 cup = 250 mL
2 cups = 1 pint = 500 mL
3 cups = 750 mL
4 cups = 1 quart = 1 L

VOLUME MEASUREMENTS (fluid)

1 fluid ounce (2 tablespoons) = 30 mL
4 fluid ounces ($1/2$ cup) = 125 mL
8 fluid ounces (1 cup) = 250 mL
12 fluid ounces ($1 1/2$ cups) = 375 mL
16 fluid ounces (2 cups) = 500 mL

WEIGHTS (mass)

$1/2$ ounce = 15 g
1 ounce = 30 g
3 ounces = 90 g
4 ounces = 120 g
8 ounces = 225 g
10 ounces = 285 g
12 ounces = 360 g
16 ounces = 1 pound = 450 g

DIMENSIONS

$1/16$ Inch = 2 mm
$1/8$ inch = 3 mm
$1/4$ inch = 6 mm
$1/2$ inch = 1.5 cm
$3/4$ inch = 2 cm
1 inch = 2.5 cm

OVEN TEMPERATURES

250°F = 120°C
275°F = 140°C
300°F = 150°C
325°F = 160°C
350°F = 180°C
375°F = 190°C
400°F = 200°C
425°F = 220°C
450°F = 230°C

BAKING PAN AND DISH EQUIVALENTS

Utensil	Size in Inches	Size in Centimeters	Volume	Metric Volume
Baking or Cake	8×8×2	20×20×5	8 cups	2 L
Pan (square or	9×9×2	23×23×5	10 cups	2.5 L
rectangular)	13×9×2	33×23×5	12 cups	3 L
Loaf Pan	8½×4½×2½	21×11×6	6 cups	1.5 L
	9×9×3	23×13×7	8 cups	2 L
Round Layer	8×1½	20×4	4 cups	1 L
Cake Pan	9×1½	23×4	5 cups	1.25 L
Pie Plate	8×1½	20×4	4 cups	1 L
	9×1½	23×4	5 cups	1.25 L
Baking Dish or			1 quart/4 cups	1 L
Casserole			1½ quart/6 cups	1.5 L
			2 quart/8 cups	2 L
			3 quart/12 cups	3 L